Mindfulness
at play

Dr Stephen McKenzie is a Senior Lecturer in Psychology at the University of Melbourne where he is developing wellbeing-related courses including a Wellbeing in Practice subject in the Master of Professional Psychology course and the Australian Psychological Society partnered Mindfulness in Clinical Practice micro certificate. He is also leading the strategic expansion of online courses. Dr McKenzie's previous mindfulness and other wellbeing-related books are: *Mindfulness for Life: The updated guide for today's world*, with Assoc. Prof. Craig Hassed, *Mindfulness at Work, Heartfulness: Beyond mindfulness, finding your real life*, all for Exisle Publishing, and *Reality Psychology: A new perspective on wellbeing, mindfulness, resilience and connection* for Springer, published in 2022.

Angela North is a psychologist with 30 years' experience working with children, adolescents and their families. Employing play therapy, which is effective at treating a range of emotional and behavioural problems, Angela is passionate about sharing strategies with parents, so that they may respond therapeutically to their own children's needs. This unique approach empowers parents to become the agent of change in their children's lives. Angela is a presenter on child mental health, writes for the Australian Psychological Society and is the Principal Consultant Psychologist for Bestchance Child Family Care.

Mindfulness at play

Parenting healthy, happy children with old wisdom and new science

Dr Stephen McKenzie and Angela North

EXISLE PUBLISHING

First published 2023

Exisle Publishing Pty Ltd
PO Box 864, Chatswood, NSW 2057, Australia
226 High Street, Dunedin, 9016, New Zealand
www.exislepublishing.com

A CiP record for this book is available from the National Library of Australia.

ISBN 978-1-922539-63-2

Designed by Mark Thacker
Typeset in Minion Pro Regular 11 on 16pt
Printed in China

This book uses paper sourced under ISO 14001 guidelines from well-
managed forests and other controlled sources.

10 9 8 7 6 5 4 3 2 1

Disclaimer
While this book is intended as a general information resource and all care
has been taken in compiling the contents, neither the authors nor the
publisher and their distributors can be held responsible for any loss, claim
or action that may arise from reliance on the information contained in this
book. As each person and situation is unique, this book should never be a
substitute for the skill, knowledge and experience of a qualified professional
dealing with the specific facts and circumstances of an individual.

Acknowledgement of Country
I acknowledge the Bunurong People as Traditional Owners and Custodians
of the land in which I live and work. I pay my respects to their Elders, past,
present, and emerging. The Traditional Owners of Country throughout
Australia are our first storytellers, with an ancient culture that can teach
us much about a mindful connection to nature, to each other, and to
ourselves.
— Angela North

To Miranda, the wonder of, and in, my life.
— Stephen

To Millie and Charlie. This book is born of my
greatest love and respect for you both. You fill my
heart, simply by being. You gift my days with your
intelligence, warmth and (especially) humour.
Even your mum writing a book about parenting
can be funny, if you look at it from the right angle.
— Angela

Contents

Introduction

Stephen McKenzie

Young people are just like young everything else — shiny, new, wonderful and full of potential. We have a short and special opportunity to help our children reach their full life potential. We can do this by giving them what is natural for the nurturers and supporters of any living thing to give — our full attention. This goes and grows with acceptance, and these both go and grow with love.

Mindfulness at Play begins, like mindfulness, like play, and like life, in wonder. It reveals, describes and demonstrates how mindfulness is really so simple that even a young person can achieve it and greatly benefit from it, naturally. Mindfulness simply involves being present and engaged in each moment of our lives. This book will help parents and their children clearly understand and practise what mindfulness is or can be.

We believe the strategies, practices and activities offered here can help mindfulness become a natural part of the way that parents parent, and that the benefits of this are substantial and far-reaching. When young people can clearly focus on their internal world in the present moment, they are better able to:

- know and communicate their experiences and needs — a critical component of emotional intelligence
- discover that they can be curious rather than overwhelmed by emotions, leading to greater emotion regulation and resilience
- increase self-acceptance and decrease shame, resulting in greater wellbeing, more effective healing from trauma, and an increase in pro-social behaviours towards others.

All we can really give anybody is our best responses to their actions, based on love and not its distortions: anxiety, impatience, anger and despair. When we are fully aware, and fully accepting of our awareness, we naturally experience our full potential. Consequently, we naturally help others experience their maximum potential.

Mindfulness at Play will help you and the children you care for experience real mindfulness and, therefore, real-life purpose, peace, happiness and love.

PART 1

Understanding mindfulness

CHAPTER 1

What mindfulness really is

Stephen McKenzie

Mindfulness can be described as a technique that is thousands of years old which has become an overnight sensation. The modern success of this ancient wellness practice is particularly apt given that it connects our minds with our bodily sensations, which naturally grounds us in our here and now reality. When we mindfully accept life's gift of the present moment, we are truly free; free of the stress that can overwhelm us when we continually want more from life than what we're currently experiencing.

Mindfulness can help parents and their children be their best, as well as do their best. When we are mindful, we stop being too busy thinking about life to really enjoy it, and we can start living naturally and well. Mindfulness is a state of simply being fully focused on whatever we are doing, including parenting, right now. It allows us to reveal and be who we really are, and to help other people, including our children, reveal who they really are.

What mindfulness *really* is

A lot has been written and discussed about mindfulness; however, it all just boils down to the practices of paying attention, being able to direct our attention, and accepting what we pay attention to. By removing our everyday distractions, mindfulness makes us fully alive. Mindfulness is actually a way *into* reality rather than *out of it* — a way of seeing things as they really are, no matter what they are.

The theory of mindfulness

Mindfulness produces benefits that can be measured scientifically. However, as with anything that has become as popular as the practice of mindfulness, there is a potential danger of some people either taking their belief too far, in that they don't require scientific evidence of any kind or, on the other end of the spectrum, disliking it so much they disregard all and any scientific evidence that it works.

We need to keep an open mind and heart about what mindfulness can do for us and our children. We therefore describe benefits of mindfulness and mindfulness practices that are supported by scientific evidence. We balance this scientific support with constant reminders of the human essence of mindfulness. An example of this is reconnecting mindfulness with the humanistic wisdom traditions, including Buddhism, which is where the concept originally emerged from. We also balance theory with practice by including descriptions of why mindfulness works and how it works, demonstrated by real-life examples.

Scientifically supported benefits of mindfulness include vital elements related to life management such as:

- better parenting
- facilitation of healthy lifestyle change
- better sleep
- pain management
- coping with major illnesses, such as cancer
- reduced allostatic load (long-term stress response).

as well as elements that are related to mental health, including:

- depression-relapse prevention
- reduced anxiety, panic disorder and stress
- management of addiction
- better emotional regulation
- greater emotional intelligence.[1]

Mindfulness can prevent people of all ages from developing mental, social or physical health problems. It can also help restore people to health if they have developed any of these problems by freeing them of their thoughts, including ones that can make them feel nervous or miserable, such as 'I should do this!', 'I should do that!', 'people expect me to do it!' or 'I have to do it soon!'. Mindfulness therefore *empowers* people and reduces dependence on long-term psychotherapy or drug therapy. It also has the important advantage of being non-harmful, non-invasive, non-threatening and non-stigma producing.

The medical and psychiatric model for helping younger people generally makes an often artificial distinction between being 'well' and 'unwell'. This is done on the basis of whether a young person has a diagnosed psychopathology or developmental disorder — such as social anxiety or dyslexia — which might be classified as being 'unwell', or whether they don't — which would be classified as being 'well'. Apart from being simplistic and often untrue, or at least less than fully true, this model can have unfortunate real-life consequences. Diagnosing a young person or anyone else with an official mental or physical condition can result in their not being offered opportunities to maximize their life. This is because official diagnoses can limit the perceptions of what a young person's real-life opportunities could involve.

The practice of mindfulness

The proof of the mindfulness pudding is the experience of mindfulness itself. All applications of mindfulness, including for parenting, are best built on our own practice of it. To understand and practise mindfulness well enough to use it to help other people, including our children, we need to understand and practise it well enough to help ourselves. This is equivalent to the instruction in pre-flight safety demonstrations for us to help ourselves to the oxygen if it's needed before helping our children to it.

It's important that we don't just move from being mindfulness pagans, who don't know about it, to being mindfulness pagans who know about it but don't practise it! We need to move from being mindfulness knowers to mindfulness livers, and this means knowing what mindfulness actually is and what its benefits really are, rather than just thinking we know what it means or what other people think it means.

To fully understand mindfulness, not only do we need to understand mindfulness practices, but we need to do them. A mindfulness practice can either be formal, which means participating in sessions such as mindful breathing or a body scan exercise, or informal, which means being mindful of — and connected to — whatever happens in our daily lives. Our informal practice of mindfulness is supported by our formal practice, and is simply:

- being fully aware of whatever is taking place in this moment
- directing our awareness to whatever is real, rather than having it distracted by what imagined realities of what might be, or was, or otherwise isn't
- accepting whatever is real.

Informal mindfulness practices
Informal mindfulness in daily living practices include:

Mindful listening — really listen to the sound of the voice of anyone who is talking to you, rather than listening to your own internal voice. Be aware of your assumptions and judgements about whoever is talking to you, as well as your expectations about what they are going to say.
Mindful communication — work towards achieving *the best* outcome with whoever you are communicating with, by practising active listening, and asking questions, rather than by trying to persuade them to agree with *your* solution. This is an ancient and effective communication practice that is known as the dialectic, or the Platonic/Socratic dialogue.

Mindful walking — really connect with all or any sense while you are moving — the feel of your feet touching the ground, the aroma in the air or the noise around you.

Mindful eating — concentrate on just the taste or texture of the food you are eating by removing any distractions around you while you eat such as watching TV, reading or moving around. Try an experiment: eat or drink anything you like with total awareness and then try eating or drinking the same thing while you are doing something else. Which experimental condition made the food taste better?

The key to unlocking any mindfulness practice and its life benefits is persistence — if you keep being still, you will stay still, naturally.

Formal mindfulness practices

This is a basic mindfulness technique which is best done for just a few minutes, at least, once a day, to gain the most benefit.

> **Be still.**
> **Be aware of your natural breath — don't try to change it, don't judge it.**
> **Just let it flow.**
> **Be aware of your in-breath (inhalation), and your out-breath (exhalation), and the space between your in-breath and out-breath.**
> **Every time that you are aware that you are thinking about anything, gently bring your awareness back to focusing on your breath.**

CHAPTER 2

Mindfulness for young people

Stephen McKenzie

'Mindfulness is a skill that can easily be, and should be, taught ... right from the beginning. It helps to foster creativity, improves academic and sporting performance and is vital for developing mental health and emotional intelligence in children.'
Mindfulness for Life, Dr Stephen McKenzie and Dr Crag Hassed[1]

The context for mindfulness for young people

There is a rapidly increasing range of mindfulness approaches, programs and apps for young people which are being offered in many countries, including in schools, pre-schools and homes. It can seem that there is so much choice in our mindfulness super-markets that it's hard to know what's best. To be of real value, these approaches need to be scientifically supported and also fit in with the practicalities of family life. It's vital for parents to understand mindfulness for young people and children of different age groups and special needs to know how it can best be applied. This chapter will assist parents, teachers and carers to help their children to transform life-changing mindfulness possibilities into life-changing mindfulness practices.

Mindfulness for infants

'The best way to make children good is to make them happy.'
Oscar Wilde

The best approach for parents of very young children, or infants, is simply to get out of the way of their natural mindfulness. This means recognizing their natural mindfulness and allowing and encouraging it. For example, if a very young child is deeply connected with an activity, no matter how seemingly irrelevant, encourage this! My daughter once sat down on the nature strip and started playing with gumnuts, while I wanted to go somewhere that I thought was much more important. Thankfully, I let go of that idea and played gumnuts. There are great opportunities for parents of children of any age, and especially of very young children, to learn mindfulness from them, as well as guide and teach them. It can be valuable for us to see mindfulness as something that we can help children to *retain* rather than something that we help them *attain*.

Very young children are inherently curious and interested in everything that they see. When we are mindful, we see things as they really are — new and exciting and interesting. This is how young children, especially very young ones, naturally experience their world. It seems new because *it is* new.

One of the best ways parents can help their children be mindful is by being a living example of it (i.e. role modelling it). Children, especially infants, watch us and what we do, and this means they can't be fooled. If we tell our children to be mindful and we don't live this way ourselves we are actually helping them to lose their natural mindfulness. Infants are mindfulness experts. They haven't developed the thoughts — theirs or those of other people, such as 'I should …!' — that get in the way of mindfulness, Infants are free of real-life distortions, such as thoughts like 'I should be a better infant' or, thankfully, 'my parents should be better parents!' Infants naturally give their total attention to whatever they are doing. They don't judge or otherwise filter reality into something other than what it actually is.

Mindful parenting, especially of very young children, is really about rewards rather than responsibilities. The smile that your baby gives you when they see you for the first time in a week, an hour or a minute, doesn't depend on what you last said or did. This is the smile of pure love, of pure delight in being alive, and in being loved and being able to love. We can respond to this non-mindfully by trying to analyse it, or we can respond by smiling back, by living in love naturally, together. Mindful parenting can be its own reward.

We can miss out on parenting treasures if we aren't really paying attention or we only focus when we think that something is going wrong, such as when our baby is crying. A great life lesson that many parents learn is that the parenting process is rapid; it can seem like suddenly our baby has grown up. The experience of parenting mindfully can help us learn great life truths, such as life isn't a stagnant pool, it's a flowing river. Mindfulness is not about avoiding mistakes — large and small — it is about realizing great life opportunities.

Mindfulness, especially with very young children, can be as easy as going with its natural flow, or as hard as always trying to work out if what we are doing is best and wondering if we should be doing something else.

Keys to mindful parenting of very young children include:

- Listening to and recognizing the needs of the child, while also noticing the opportunities to communicate with them mindfully. This is true for all children and especially for very young children, because they have no other choice than to communicate with us naturally, as they don't have language! Thankfully, we don't start off being parents of teenagers, who can challenge us with complicated reasons for doing or not doing what we want them to do!
- Communicating deeply and honestly, even, and especially with, someone who can't talk back to us with words. Real communication happens only when we are fully present and connected in the moment.
- Attending fully to the reality of a moment. This allows us to respond to a very young person's subtle needs, as well as to their obvious ones, including affirmation, stimulation and relaxation.

A great thing about being the parent of anyone, and especially a parent of a very young person, is that they help us naturally transition from an attitude of 'What's in it for me?' to one of 'What can I give?' This can greatly help us to become a fully conscious human being. If an infant crying out for milk or love in the middle of the night doesn't wake us up, what will?

LIVING EXAMPLES

When my daughter was a young baby, I had an instinct to communicate with her deeply and did this by simply holding her and looking into her eyes. To my surprise and delight she responded by looking back into my eyes, for a long time. It felt as if she clearly understood my unspoken language of love, and that I didn't need to do or say anything else ...

An example of not-so-mindful parenting involved giving my baby a bath on the living room floor one night while also watching a football match on TV. My connection with the reality of what I was doing was totally lost when my favourite football team kicked a particularly spectacular goal. In less time than it took for the goal to be shown again on a replay, my baby slopped most of her bathwater all over the carpet and was trying to drink the rest of it.

Mindfulness for children

'The way we talk to our children becomes
their inner voice.'
Peggy O'Mara

If people were once mindful and aren't now, what went wrong? Psychology offers us many descriptions of people, including children, who have lost their mental and emotional way, including in its diagnoses of clinical conditions. It is simpler and more valuable, however, to see potential ways home, no matter how far away from it we think we are. It doesn't really matter why children lose their natural mindfulness; it's easy to do in a world where mass media minds rule, and don't often rule well. All we can do as parents is help children when they lose their mindfulness by bringing them and ourselves, back to it, as many times as necessary.

Children start off their lives feeling a deep sense of unity with everyone and everything in their universe. Then something happens that results in losing this, and they experience a separate ego, feel non-unified and at times alone, anxious or angry. This phenomenon of individual ego development is sometimes referred to as the 'terrible twos' but it often starts earlier. What else happens at about this age?

The development of language greatly affected the development of the human species, and it also greatly affects the development of individual humans. Suddenly, it becomes possible for very young humans to start thinking and talking and experiencing complex reactions to people and events. Examples of this phenomenon, which can lead to a sense of separation rather than unity, include when children begin saying things like, 'I prefer this' or 'I don't like that.' However, we can help children preserve and/or return to their mindful innocence and sense of inner unity by role modelling our own sense of mindfulness. We can explain, and also demonstrate by our actions, that there is actually much more important stuff than their mind-made thoughts and other people's mind-made thoughts. What's actually more important is what's beyond this, such as a deeper life meaning, and feelings of unity and love. Ancient life wisdom traditions all have the equivalent of a theory of mind, and practices that explore and encourage this. For example, Christianity emphasizes love and forgiveness; Buddhism emphasizes compassion and letting go; Hinduism emphasizes an absolute unified reality that can always be returned to, in its doctrine of reincarnation — the belief that people and ideas evolve by being reborn.

It's vital that we keep giving children who have begun developing and using spoken language more than words. We need to communicate with them on a deeper level than persuasion, coercion, or any other kind of individual self-interest. An example of such communication could mean being with our child and giving them our unconditional attention, love and the enjoyment of just existing together, without having to play any role.

It's vital for truly mindful parenting to not put it off. If we wait until *later*, or *when we are less busy*, we can miss out on the great life and love opportunity that parenting really is. How long does it really take to be with anyone? What's more important than spending time and practising being in the moment with our children? Real-life examples of this could include walking them to school when we can; asking them about anything that's important to them, or even that's not; or sharing their interests as well as helping them share ours. Just like in the messages of many parents who left connecting deeply with their children until it was too late, such as Harry Chapin's potentially prophetic song 'Cat's in the Cradle', don't wait until it's too late. Do it *now*. Be it *now*. Being a total parent doesn't mean pandering to our child's every whim or smothering them with so much of anything that they can't digest it; it just means keeping on coming back to total connection. Real life, including real parenting life, is about experiencing happy and enlightening surprises, as well as disasters.

LIVING EXAMPLES

An old friend of my mother had a large number of children. One day she took them to an agricultural show and bought them all ice creams. When she handed out the ice creams there was one left over, which meant that one of her children was missing! The child was eventually found, and a lesson was learned. This is both an example of the mindlessness that can cause a child to be lost, and an example of mindfulness in realizing that a child was missing!

I very recently experienced my own moment of mindless parenting when I was so engrossed in contributing to a chapter on mindful parenting for this book that I forgot to collect my daughter from her tennis lesson! All turned out well enough in the end, as it often does, when I managed to collect her from her lesson and learned my own before it was too late ...

A universal example of mindful parenting is the act of crea-tion — of games, adventures, stories — and possibilities. A particular example of this is helping my daughter develop mindfulness by guiding her mindful copying of wise say-ings every morning. Another example is when I invent and play games with my daughter, particularly in the Covid-19 lockdown, such as the game of 'tosh', a hybrid of tennis and squash that can be played against a backyard or courtyard wall ...

Mindfulness for teenagers

'When I was a boy of fourteen, my father was so ignorant I could hardly stand to have the old man around. But when I got to be 21, I was astonished at how much the old man had learned in seven years.'

Mark Twain

Being a teenager can be challenging, as anyone who has ever known one, parented one or remembers being one, may know. Teenagers are in a state of transition: between being children and being adults, between being dependent and being independent, and between needing to listen and needing to talk. Teenagers need to somehow learn to balance the experience of being an individual with the experience of being deeply connected with other individuals, and this can result in turbulence. Breaking through the separation sound barrier can present great challenges to teenagers themselves and also to their parents, teachers and others. Part of the turbulence is the great challenge that teenagers must develop and assert their emerging adult identity, while also conforming to the behaviours and expectations of their tribe.

It's a well-known paradox that teenagers often think they are rebelling against their parents and society, when in fact they are really conforming to what their friends are doing and thinking or what *they think* they are doing and thinking! Teenagers typically don't realize that if everyone is rebelling in the same way, they are actually conforming. It can be valuable to show, rather than tell, your teenagers that they don't always need to conform, especially if it has the potential to make others, including themselves, miserable. Destructive group behaviour, from taking drugs to serial complaining — group non-acceptance of reality — often begins as an unconscious act of group conformity. It's actually more fun for teenagers, or any of us, to really connect with and enjoy the ups and downs of life than it is to be constantly cool!

It can be valuable for parents of teenagers to keep bearing in mind that all things pass, including teenage turbulence. Eventually, even great barriers can be broken through, and peace of mindfulness restored. It can also be very valuable to bear in mind that there are reasons for what teenagers do or don't do, just as there are reasons for what all of us do or don't do. Even if there doesn't seem to be any sense at all in what your or some-one else's teenager has just done, it often makes perfect sense to them. The more mindful, patient and understanding that we are, or can convincingly pretend to be, the more likely we will be to help transform great teenage-transition challenges into great life-growth opportunities.

The reasons why teenagers do what they do include neu-rophysiological reasons,[2] as well as psychological, social and philosophical reasons. For example, neuroimaging has revealed that our brain structure isn't fully developed until early adult-hood, with boys' brains not fully maturing until they reach their mid-twenties, and girls' brains fully maturing at about twenty. Teenagers have been shown to exhibit increased neural reactivity to emotions and rewards: they are more life sensitive. This can explain why teenagers and people in their early twenties have been known to do what other people might think of as seem-ingly odd things. Psychologists like to talk about the need for the development of self-awareness and emotion-regulation. We can talk more universally, however, about the need for the develop-ment of self-knowledge and mindfulness. We don't need to be theoretical experts in anything to help our teenagers and our-selves become really connected.

Our current generation of teenagers might seem like they are the most challenging of all time; however, every generation of teenagers has been seen as the most challenging of all time. James Dean famously starred in *Rebel Without a Cause* in 1955, for example, a very influential movie about particularly problem-atic and confused suburban, middle-class teenagers.

Modern teenagers do, however, have special challenges,

including living in a world and communities that are increasingly virtual, not to mention living with pandemics and other highly contagious challenging life situations. It is especially important now for parents of teenagers to be realistically positive about what's happening in their teenagers' lives, and to help them grow with, rather than shrink from, their great life challenges.

Helping our teenagers be mindfully aware and accepting doesn't mean helping them be cool. It means helping them be fully conscious, fully connected and fully alive. This means assisting them to make good life decisions, large and small, and helping them be part of any group. In *A New Earth*, author Eckhart Tolle told us what we might already know, and not want to, that teenagers can resent their parents.[3] According to Eckhart Tolle, a lot of this resentment arises because many parents are 'inauthentic'. As parents we can get so trapped in the role of being a parent and trying to play it well that we don't simply develop genuinely real — human, mindful — relationships with our children. Above all, we need to treat our teenagers as people who have the potential to be as wonderful on the outside as they are in their essence. This means really communicating with them from the heart, rather than just talking to them from the mind, and fully accepting them and their real value, no matter what!

A PARENTING STORY FROM THE HEART

When a well-known writer was told that he was dying of cancer, his wife decided to tell their young children what was really happening, and not try to 'protect them'. She also decided that she would tell them children's stories that included great life challenges, darkness and ways out of or beyond the darkness – essentially classical children's stories. She did this because she found out that many children's stories authors had great challenges in their lives, which writing helped them to understand and transform. She also did this because she believed that darkness is real, and so is light.

PART 2

The benefits of mindfulness

CHAPTER 3

The secret password to your child's inner world

Angela North

There is a concept in psychology that we all need just one person in our childhood who truly sees us — so that we feel deeply heard, understood and loved. We carry this person's belief in us throughout life; their wisdom and acceptance is a salve against the misguided commentary of others. This person may not be our parent. It may be a grandparent, foster parent, neighbour, aunt or teacher. So while this book refers to 'parents', we refer to *all* the caretakers of children who come in many, many forms. You are here, and that speaks volumes about your intention to be that important person in a child's life.

First: choose your own adventure

Depending on life circumstances, you may find yourself fully able and motivated to learn something new. Or not. If you are a single parent of young children, your learning and reflection time might be minimal. Perhaps your relationship with your teen has been fraught for so long your cup feels quite empty. You might be managing significant life challenges, such as a relationship breakdown or health problems. You might be grieving a significant loss. I encourage you to reflect on how much you can currently manage. If the very idea of learning new strategies has you running for the hills, then please don't despair — there is something in here for everyone. From small steps to giant leaps, there will be tools that require very little brain power and tools for those who are ready for more. You will know which strategies are right for you because the ones that match your current capacity will excite and energize you. Hope, curiosity and optimism have a way of doing that. This book's subtitle includes 'old wisdom and new science'. Since mindfulness has stood the test of time, each strategy within this book will be here for you, whenever you are ready. It is important to honour your own capacity in this moment. You get to choose.

The benefits

Mindfulness can be embedded in everyday interactions through a key skill called 'empathic reflections'. This skill requires us to pay close attention to our child's wishes, needs and emotions, to reflect our understanding using our own words, and to do this with calmness and empathy.

This chapter will help you understand the *how* — how mindful parenting responses will lead to many benefits for you and your child. In later chapters of the book, you will find all the practical details and examples, so that you can begin your own mindful practice.

LIVING EXAMPLE

Amelia builds a block tower, knocks it over, covers her ears and cries. She raises a chubby hand to her mother, presenting the offending block for their inspection. Her mother responds with empathy, using her words to show Amelia she understands. She could have responded based on her own ideas about resilience, saying something like 'you're okay' or 'never mind'. Instead, she reflects Amelia's feelings, saying calmly, 'That gave you a surprise! It was too noisy, and you wanted me to see '

Amelia is only two, but her mother's empathic tone makes the message clear. Satisfied that she was understood, Amelia's body relaxes. She releases a big breath, and happily returns to her play.

Amelia is demonstrating two years' of accumulated knowledge, much of it gained through play. In a relatively short period of time, Amelia has learned to coordinate her eyes and hands, to manage sensory input by covering her ears, and to seek her mother's attention and comfort so that emotional balance is restored.

In short, Amelia is building valuable life skills, particularly her ability to regulate her emotions. Her mother's mindful response is deceptively simple.

When Amelia's mother tunes into Amelia's experience, rather than her own thoughts or ideas, Amelia is learning to:

- tune inwards rather than remain focused on the blocks
- notice and label the feelings ('I was surprised/frightened by the noise')
- try a strategy for self-calming (seeking validation from a parent)
- discover that it is safe to seek comfort (the response was caring, not dismissive).

The calmness of her mother's response has another important, implicit message. It is a profoundly effective way to teach children that feelings are nothing to be afraid of. Many children (and adults) who suffer from anxiety are more afraid of the anxious feeling than the perceived source of anxiety itself. As Amelia will eventually discover, like clouds in the sky, feelings come and go.

As young children, we are naturally mindful — you only have to watch an infant study their fingers with the focus of a scientist, or a toddler's tantrum evaporate at the appearance of a favourite relative. This is focused attention, with every feeling experienced in the moment, then left behind without judgement. In the example above, Amelia wastes no time worrying about her actions, such as whether she is clumsy, noisy or naughty. She is free to experiment, learn from failure, improve her problem-solving skills and her ability to manage the ebb and flow of feelings.

Over time, Amelia will develop language, and begin to internally verbalise her thoughts and ideas, her experiences, and other people's comments and behaviours. This inner voice will reflect Amelia's own temperament, her life experiences, and the kind of care she has received from her parents and others. Indeed, this inner voice can become a 'valuable self-regulation and motivational tool',[1] helping Amelia cope with big feelings and impulses, and propelling her to further exploration of her world. However, if Amelia's inner voice is particularly critical, it will dampen her natural ability to stay in the present moment — instead, spending too much time fretting about the past, or worrying about the future. An internal voice that is harsh and judgemental will erode her willingness to experience challenging feelings, or to persist through failure towards her goals. As US industrialist Henry Ford once famously said, 'Whether you think you can, or think you can't, you're right.' In other words, attitude has a big role to play in success or failure.

We want Amelia — and all children — to inherit an internal voice that sounds less like a punishing critic and more like a life coach: full of compassion, authenticity and belief in their ability to persist, overcome and succeed. Where does this voice come from? As mentioned earlier, it originates partly from the child's own temperament — everyone is 'wired' uniquely at birth, and this can make life easier or harder. But life events and parent responses play a powerful part — and it is the latter that is the focus here, because it is where parents have the greatest influence.

As parents, we can strongly influence the inner voice our child develops, so that the dialogue in their head sounds like an honest, encouraging, motivating life coach. To be even more specific, here is what the research tells us about the social and emotional benefits of mindfulness:

Benefits for parents

As any flight attendant will tell you, the best way to care for others is to put your own oxygen mask on first. Parents who practise mindfulness benefit from greater wellbeing, and improved relationships with partners and children. According to a recent review of mindful parenting outcomes[2] these benefits may include:

- Greater optimism, improved mental health, fewer self-blaming thoughts.
- Fewer automatic thoughts and reactions.
- More realistic expectations of children that fit with the child's age and development.
- Improved confidence in their ability to parent.
- Use of more effective parenting practices, such as calm responses, consistent discipline and logical reasoning to teach social and emotional skills.
- An increase in warm, trusting, respectful parent–child interactions.

Benefits for children

Research into the benefits of mindfulness for families is considerable, showing significant changes for children and adolescents.[3]

Importantly, these benefits appear to be universal, observed in research across the globe:

- Better ability to manage emotions (shorter, fewer tantrums, calmer responses).
- A healthier relationship with themselves — greater self-awareness, self-esteem, confidence.
- Improved relationships with others, including parents, family and friends.
- Greater ability to resist peer pressure.
- Fewer behavioural and psychological problems (including children and adolescents diagnosed with ADHD, Oppositional-Defiant Disorder, Conduct Disorder and Autism Spectrum Disorder).
- Improved capacity to focus, remember and learn.
- Less likely to use illicit substances.
- Greater openness and honesty with parents.

An additional benefit: safety

The last point in the list above — greater openness — is especially worth exploring. Certainly, an open, honest relationship with a loving parent makes for a more joyful, satisfying family life. But it also has another, equally important function: it can keep children and adolescents *safe*. In fact, mindfulness offers what psychologists call a 'protective factor'.

It goes without saying that we want our children to be safe. Some of us will work hard — perhaps even too hard, to achieve this. As Foster Cline and Jim Fay wrote in *Parenting with Love and*

Logic,[4] where they first coined the term 'helicopter parent', such a parent is forever observing and rescuing their child, whenever small troubles arise. But there is a price to pay, in both parent wellbeing and child resilience. We rob children of opportunities for age-appropriate risk-taking (where self-awareness, resilience and life skills are learned) and the experience of natural consequences (where accountability is learned).

While we know in our hearts that we cannot create a perfect world for our children, we try. Because in our mind's eye, we are recalling all the challenging things that happened to us. In our bodies we are remembering what it felt like to be bullied, experience racism, hear the sharp comment from a teacher or friend. A lifetime of comments and actions that moulded our view of ourselves, or perhaps 'confirmed' a fear about ourselves. These experiences can attach to our sense of identity, and we may believe they are true, *simply because they originated at a time when we were too young to question them.* So many painful cuts, little and big. And then we have children, and we want to protect them from *all* of that, because we have barely learned to tolerate our own experiences.

Yet, at the same time, we know the truth: that at some point, we must let our children out into the world. While cultures differ in how much and how quickly they encourage independence, all parents must eventually make the transition from full responsibility for a newborn's every need to those ever-increasing moments when we must wave goodbye — and hope they are going to thrive — as they head to kindergarten, school, a party, a part-time job, a date, a driving test, a camping trip or perhaps to university.

Mindfulness offers us an alternative approach, with the aim of building up our children's own abilities to keep themselves safe. Mindful parenting helps children build their own internal 'life coach' who travels with them wherever they go. This inner guide is neither critical nor overly afraid, but rather self-aware, able to weigh risks and rewards, and confident about who to turn to when help is needed.

Let's think about some of the common behaviours that increase risk for children. Keeping secrets can be a risk, because parents cannot intervene, advise or support if they don't know what's happening. Succumbing to pressure from peers or adults can also be a risk. The most common risks are:

- lying/keeping secrets
- succumbing to peer pressure
- impulsive decision making
- ignoring inner warnings.

Young children and adolescents alike are vulnerable to the influence of others for many reasons, including a wish to fit in, be liked, and simply because they don't yet know their own minds. Where a child lacks a 'sense of self' — a relatively clear self-image that includes personality traits, abilities, likes, dislikes and a moral code — other, stronger personalities can easily step in. And most children are vulnerable to the power difference between an adult and child, particularly as parenting (and cultures generally) emphasize obedience over trusting our own instincts.

In later chapters you will see how mindful parenting offers a trust-building response to children's worries and mistakes. These responses reduce the need for secrets. Because, while learning how to do life, every child makes poor choices and mistakes. If your child discovers they can share anything with you, and receive calm, mindful responses, they are more likely to keep talking when it matters most. Put simply, mindful parenting builds trusting relationships, keeping the channels of communication open (even through adolescence!), so that you continue to be a valued source of guidance and support.

CHAPTER 4

Attention and learning benefits

Stephen McKenzie

'What we give our attention to grows.'

Maharishi Mahesh Yogi

When people think of mindfulness and its benefits they tend to think of reduced stress and improved wellbeing. However, mindfulness also has great benefits for school and work performance, because being able to focus our attention helps us really concentrate on what we are doing. As a consequence, mindfulness helps both young and older people to learn — at school and at work — and to learn well and enjoyably. To help our children and teenagers achieve its best benefits, it's important that we understand how mindfulness helps learning. Mindfulness is much more than an increasingly popular way of helping people to relax, or to 'chill out, or even 'zone out'. Mindfulness actually helps people learn to 'zone in'. When a child or a teenager develops mindful attention and a mindful attitude of natural wonder, curiosity and playfulness with whatever they are attending to, they are in the best possible learning space, no matter what their formal learning ability is.

Attention

Attention is like a light, always shining on *something*. It can be focused like a laser or widened like a sunset. When we focus our attention, we develop concentration. When we widen the focus, we develop awareness. Mindfulness helps children, teenagers and all of us to do both.

When we focus our attention on anything, whether it is something good, bad or neutral, we become more aware of it. Have you ever lain in bed at night unable to get to sleep and then tried to stop your thoughts? Did this help? Have you ever been in a stressful situation and tried to stop thinking about it? Did you notice that the more attention you gave to trying to stop your thoughts, the more important they became, or the larger and louder they seemed? Did you notice that giving attention to thoughts made you more aware of them?

Here's an interesting exercise for you to try. There was once a special entrance requirement for joining a particular club: spend a minute *not* thinking about polar bears. Now you have a go and see if you would pass the entry test ...

Any luck? The *not* thinking club must have been a very exclusive one! Many people believe that being mindful means being able to stop your thoughts. It doesn't. It means being able to stop the potentially distracting and damaging effects of your thoughts by just observing them. The harder we try to not notice something, the more we focus our attention on it, and the more we notice it.

Trying to block something that flows as naturally as attention does creates problems. Much like damming a wall in a river, it stems a natural force that can be emotional or cognitive. Directing our attention flow, however, can be extremely valuable because if we focus it on whatever we are trying to learn, for example, it will grow. We have a choice between watering the weeds of our minds with our attention or watering our mind garden.

Whatever we focus fully on becomes increasingly hardwired in our brains and bodies, and increasingly easy to keep doing. This is the fundamental basis of learning anything. When we are giving and directing our full attention to something, we are fully conscious, fully engaged, fully alive and, as a result, we are total life learners. Whether we direct our full attention to the here-and-now reality of our sensory experiences, or let it be interfered with by ideas about the past and future, determines what pathways are strengthened in our brains. Giving full attention creates new connections in areas of our brains such as the prefrontal cortex and hippocampus, which strengthen learning. Being distracted creates new connections in our default mode network and amygdala, which strengthen habitual stress reactions. What we focus our attention on grows.

The challenge
Not being able to give and direct our full attention is growing problem, and a source of stress in our work, schoolwork and relationships.[1] There is a myth in our culture that it's good to be busy, and that multi-tasking leads to increased efficiency. Research shows, however, that multi-tasking leads to doing

many things badly. An article published in the *Harvard Business Review* referred to *hyperkinetic* workplaces,[2] which lead to stress, and psychological and physical problems. 'Hyper' literally means 'over' and 'kinetic' refers to movement, so hyperkinetic accurately describes the pace of modern life, which is progressing so quickly that it's increasingly hard to keep up with. This starts in school, where many children (and educators) are creating overactive and mindless ways of operating.

The inability of adults to give full attention to what they are doing and who they are doing it with can lead to workplace burnout, fatigue and conflict. Outside of the workplace it can lead to psychological stress, accidents, communication breakdowns and even relationship break-ups. The inability of children and teenagers to give their attention fully can lead to learning problems or to learning-associated social problems.

Attention Deficit and Hyperactivity Disorder (ADHD) is an extreme form of inability for someone to fully direct their attention. There are less extreme and more common forms of this whose manifestations can include a lack of engagement with schoolwork and with school itself. ADHD is currently diagnosed in anywhere between 1 in 1000 and 1 in 10 of children, depending on which country the child lives in. It is now accepted that there is a strong medical/biological component to ADHD; however, there can also be environmental contributing factors, such as excessive screen time in early childhood which may increase the risk of ADHD later on.

Mindfulness can be useful in the prevention of conditions that involve a lack of ability to direct attention. A meta-analysis of the results of ten studies conducted by Molly Cairncross and Carlin

Miller,[3] showed that mindfulness-based therapies can reduce the symptoms of ADHD, which supports the value of its use at least as an adjunctive treatment.

When mindfulness programs are given to children with complex learning or social issues it should be done with care and only with the full cooperation of the children and their parents. It can be useful to start with informal mindfulness practices, such as pausing before activities, before building these up to formal programs.

The solution

We need to recognize that there is a reason why increasing rates of children, teenagers and adults are experiencing clinical and sub-clinical attention problems. One of these reasons could be the busy way we are living and our life priorities. For example, our attempts to multi-task have unintended destructive consequences. We are neurologically incapable of focusing on more than one complex thing at a time. We can do two simple tasks concurrently — for example, walking down the street and bouncing a ball — usually without falling in a hole. Most people can manage this. Most people can also do a simple and a complex task, such as walking down the street and talking on a mobile phone, also usually without falling in a hole. When we try to do two or more complex things at a time however — for example, driving and talking on the phone — we are four times more likely to crash. If we do this in a driving simulator our driving is impaired as much as if we had a .08 blood alcohol reading.[4] Students who try to multi-task while studying impair their study performance significantly. We generally don't notice this happening, as we do it so often, but if we were to pay full attention to the costs of losing our attention, we would see the damage that it causes.

Dividing our attention by multi-tasking results in us achieving less, not more, and doing it less well. For example, if your child is studying but also talking to someone at the same time, even if it is a study buddy, the effectiveness of the study is diminished. Attention-switching (giving our full attention to only one thing at a time) results in better learning and also improved emotional benefits.[5] Distractedness, multi-tasking and other forms of mass-mindlessness result in poor learning and can cause or add to emotional problems. A recent study of the effects on young people watching two screens at the same time showed a correlation with behavioural problems, as well as learning problems.[6] Unfortunately, many teachers, as well as parents, are modelling mass mindless rather than mindful behaviours.

To help increase our children's and teenagers' ability to think clearly and retain information, we need to encourage them to give their attention to one thing at a time. This involves us resisting the temptation to always be glued to our digital devices, pay full attention when we talk to or do things with them, and generally model mindful behaviour as much as we can. We need to be aware of the amount of time that our children and teenagers spend in 'virtual reality', and of the effects this can have on them. We need to encourage children and teenagers to spend more time in reality and fully sharing it with other people through talking, listening and playing.

The evidence

There is growing scientific evidence that mindfulness helps children and teenagers with clinical attention problems, as well as with general attention problems. A study by clinical psychologist Saskia van der Oord and colleagues in Belgium showed that parent ratings of the ADHD behaviour of their children significantly improved after eight weeks of mindfulness training.[7] There was also a significant improvement in mindful awareness, and in parents' stress levels and their own over-activity. Another study by Eva van de Weijer-Bergsma and colleagues showed that parents' ratings of their children's ADHD behaviour, and also their executive functioning improved after eight weeks of group-based mindfulness training.[8]

Mindfulness has been shown to significantly improve performance on computerised sustained-attention tasks and improve the ability to select goal-relevant information when it is mixed with irrelevant information. This results in decreased distractibility and increased ability to pay attention.[9]

TAKE-HOME AND TAKE-TO-SCHOOL MINDFUL ATTENTION TIPS

Growing up in our complex, disconnected and virtual world is reducing our ability to really pay full attention, and therefore diminishes our capacity to retain information and think clearly. These problems are particularly damaging to children and teenagers. There are simple ways that we can help children and teenagers, as well as ourselves, benefit from paying real attention, including:

Reading books rather than screens. This stabilizes attention and results in improved academic performance.[10]

Spending more time communicating face-to-face rather than texting. This has been shown to reduce distractibility.[11]

Paying attention to whatever naturally interests us, cultivating our natural curiosity. This is central to mindfulness and is the opposite of living life habitually and taking things for granted. This leads to deeper engagement and therefore better learning.

Recognizing that multi-tasking is an illusion and decreases wellbeing and performance.

Learning

Learning continues throughout our lifespan. We have opportunities to learn at any age; however, children and teenagers have especially great opportunities to learn — academically, socially and emotionally. The learning styles, mindsets and ways of paying attention that children encounter in the first years of their lives, including the modelling by parents and other vital adults, deeply affects how — and how well — they will learn and live throughout their whole lives.

The challenge

Our society today is making it harder for children and teenagers to find their way in it, let alone reach their full potential as human beings. Learning difficulties appear to be getting more common and there has been debate about whether this is caused by better diagnosis, broader diagnostic definitions or even psychosocial factors.[12] Dementia has meant basically the same thing since the seventeenth century; however, definitions of learning difficulties have changed constantly, and often mean different things in different countries.

There is clear evidence that learning difficulties are closely associated with emotional and behavioural difficulties in young people.[13] Extreme forms of learning problems include those related to serious emotional, social, behavioural and attention problems. As with children and teenagers' emotional and social problems, their learning problems fall on a spectrum from minor difficulties all the way through to clinically significant disorders that can seriously disrupt their lives. Ultimately, though, it is unfortunate if *any* child isn't learning or living as well as they have the potential to.

The solution

Helping children and teenagers develop mindfulness by providing examples, sharing mindful activities with them and teaching them formal (meditation) and informal (everyday) mindfulness practices helps them to learn, anything, as well as possible — emotionally, socially and academically. This reduces their chance of developing any type of learning disorders by helping them develop a wide range of learning mechanisms and reduces their likelihood of developing mood disturbances, such as anxiety that can lead to learning difficulties.

Children and teenagers need primary and fully real experiences as well as secondary and virtual ones to help their learning. Primary or deep life experiences include playing in and enjoying nature or otherwise engaging with their natural environment, and wholeheartedly engaging with their senses rather than spending increasing amounts of time in and on screens and other reality filters. Full engagement with their senses allows young people to optimally develop the neural connections that enable emotional, social and academic learning. We naturally learn most effectively by playing games, sport and other recreational activities. Playfulness and curiosity can also be encouraged in classrooms, and this improves learning outcomes. Encouraging young people's innate playfulness helps them to access their inherent mindfulness. The natural antidote to children and teenagers spending too much time staring at computer and television screens is encouraging them to spend more time being physically active and outside. Children and teenagers learn best by doing, and by being and doing with other people, and by doing one thing at a time.

The evidence

Many scientific studies have shown that mindfulness improves mood problems that impair learning. A study by Beauchemin and colleagues,[14] for example, showed that mindfulness reduces the anxiety levels and improves social skills of children and teenagers with learning disorders, and enhances their learning capacities. Another study found that mindfulness decreases tendencies to avoid unwanted experiences, which improves mood and resilience and therefore reduces an important barrier to learning.[15] Importantly, recent studies have shown that parents can administer mindfulness programs to children that improve their learning ability.[16]

As well as the considerable evidence showing that mindfulness improves young people's emotional and social states, which in turn improves their learning, there is also considerable evidence to show that mindfulness practices can directly enhance learning-related cognitive attributes. Mrazek and colleagues,[17] for example, showed that mindfulness improves working memory capacity, a vital aspect of learning, and therefore results in better reading ability. A large meta-analytic study of the emotional and social benefits of mindfulness described in the next chapter also showed that mindfulness improves emotion associated cognitive capacities, as measured by before and after mindfulness intervention improvements in academic grades.[18]

TAKE-HOME AND TAKE-TO-SCHOOL MINDFUL LEARNING TIPS

Mindfulness helps young people focus on what they want and need to focus on and helps them deal with distractions. Better focus leads to better learning outcomes. Cultivating an attitude of acceptance – another central quality of mindfulness – also helps attention and learning by reducing reactivity. Curiosity can be cultivated through mindfulness practice, and this increases young people's engagement and therefore attention, and consolidates their learning and increases their understanding. Cultivating an attitude of playfulness and experimentation makes learning fun as well as optimally effective. Here are some ways to enable this:

Gain the profound attention and learning benefits of mindfulness ourselves, and model them!

Use formal mindfulness programs to help children and teenagers retain and restore their natural mindfulness. We can also use these programs to help build their natural immunity to the many emotional stresses and strains of our modern world. Mindfulness helps children's and teenagers' social and emotional development, learning, and ability to direct their attention by protecting these natural capacities, from their own and other people's unhelpful ideas about how they can be improved.

Recognize, encourage and work with children's and teenagers' natural interests and creativity as a way of demonstrating or facilitating a sense of mindfulness. If a child shows an interest in something, they will naturally focus on it.

Mindfulness is a powerful, natural and economical way of helping parents and schools enable young people to maximize their learning. It does this by helping them regulate attention, deal with emotions, manage frustration and increase self-motivation.[19] As well as the obvious benefits for academic learning and performance, mindfulness also helps young people develop into awake, ethical human beings. As Adele Diamond, professor of neuroscience at the University of British Columbia, nicely puts it:[20]

'Academic achievement, social and emotional competence and physical and mental health are fundamentally and multiply interrelated. The best and most efficient way to foster any of these is to foster all of them.'

CHAPTER 5

Making friends with reality

Stephen McKenzie

'The most precious gift we can offer others
is our presence.
When mindfulness embraces those we love,
they will bloom like flowers.'

Thich Nhat Hanh

Wellbeing and resilience

Wellbeing is more than not having a diagnosed physical or psychological illness; it is a state of physical, psychological and essential wholeness, and it is our natural state.

Resilience is our ability to maintain and bounce back to our natural physical, psychological and essential wholeness when things go wrong.

The challenge

Many of us today are experiencing symptoms of mindless overload and mindful underload, such as stress, anxiety and depression. These interfere with our state of natural wellbeing and resilience. Children and teenagers are also increasingly experiencing high levels of these conditions, sometimes in similar forms to adult versions. Children and teenagers are often even less able to recognize and articulate their emotional problems than adults are. An important benefit of mindfulness is that it can solve these problems, whether they can be articulated or not. Even more importantly, it can help build the resilience to prevent, as well as return, from these states.

The solution

The mindful response to children's and teenagers' emotional and behavioural problems, or potential problems, is as simple as making friends with reality. Mindfulness can reduce and improve established mood disorders, and also nip mild disorders in their developmental buds. This is because mindfulness improves children's and teenagers' ability to be aware and accepting of what actually *is* happening inside or outside of them — right here and right now — without repressing, without avoiding, without brooding.

The evidence

A large meta-analysis study (a single study that analyses the results of many studies) provided scientific evidence that mindfulness helps children and teenagers develop (and maintain) a wide range of wellbeing-related positive emotional capacities. The study was conducted in Germany and analysed the results of 24 scientific studies conducted around the world, eleven of them unpublished, on the effectiveness of a range of mindfulness interventions offered in schools.[1] The mindfulness interventions were provided by seven teachers, fifteen non-teachers (mindfulness trainers) and two combined teachers/mindfulness trainers.

The results of the meta-analysis showed that mindfulness improves children's and adolescents' behaviour and emotional states in the following areas:

- Ruminative thinking style — reducing the time they spend mentally chewing over events rather than fully responding to the present moment.
- Negative emotions and behaviour.
- Emotional regulation difficulties.
- Somatic reactions (negative bodily responses).
- Test anxiety.
- Clinical anxiety and depression.
- Resilience.
- Wellbeing.
- Self-esteem.

Scientific studies using Mindfulness Behavioural Interventions (MBIs) with students who have serious emotional issues have found that these techniques improve depression and anxiety levels.[2] Scientific studies have also shown that mindfulness helps children and adolescents by:

- reducing their stress levels
- improving their stress-related physical problems
- improving their hostility and emotional discomfort.[3]

TAKE-HOME AND TAKE-TO-SCHOOL MINDFUL WELLBEING AND RESILIENCE TIPS

Mindfulness doesn't just help children and teenagers who have lost their natural wellbeing and/or ability to maintain it. It helps *all* children and teenagers develop and maintain the emotional wellness and resilience that is increasingly vital to help them live as well as they can, and to protect them from the potential harms of a challenging world. The distinction between clinical and 'normal' levels of unnatural emotional states is becoming more and more blurred. A solution involving mindfulness is becoming increasingly clearer.

- Help the young people in your life to use mindfulness to develop optimal wellbeing and resilience by using mindfulness yourself.
- Physician, heal thyself; parent, help thyself!
- Mindfully encourage young people to see wellbeing as a whole system that includes psychological and social wellbeing, as well as physical wellbeing.
- Mindfully encourage young people to develop natural resilience by seeing life as a stage play — to be whole-heartedly connected with and enjoyed, rather than 'won'.

Relationships

Ubuntu is a philosophy practised by some African people that can be summed up in this standard greeting and response:

'How are you?'

'I am well if you are well!'

Ubuntu is based on the understanding that your sense of yourself is shaped by your relationships with others. No matter what we think, we are naturally deeply connected to other people: our family, friends and teachers. We exist relative to other people, and if we are not really well connected, we are not really well.

Similarly, the seventeenth-century poet John Donne famously wrote:

> **No man is an island,**
> **Entire of itself.**
> **Each is a piece of the continent,**
> **A part of the main.**
> **If a clod be washed away by the sea,**
> **Europe is the less ...**

Donne's poem clearly expresses the ideal of mindfulness connection: no one can be entirely self-sufficient or exist solely by themselves without some sort of connection to others, and to be isolated from such a connection is to be diminished.

The challenge

There are many examples of behaviours and actions that reveal that someone is disconnected and not fully in the present. In adults this disconnection can manifest as uncontrolled desires for more material objects and intangible rewards, such as money and success. However, instead of satisfying the desire, this actually leads to more thinking, more stress, and less peace of mind. Swapping the peace and happiness of being fully connected with what we have (present moment reality), and who we share it with, for the stress of wanting what we don't have and will never have (the past and the future) is a bad deal. In children and teenagers, a disconnection from reality can manifest as a desire for more approval, or sporting or fashion success, or for some other desire that acts as a substitute to what we all really crave — love.

The solution

Mindfulness helps young people develop good relationships, particularly when these are modelled by parents and carers. Mindfulness creates a feeling of connection and when we feel connected, we are less likely to express any sense of isolation from other people as anger or anxiety. When we experience full connection with an experience or a relationship, we can swim with, rather than against, the flow of our life circumstances. When we are going with our flow we can focus on and learn from reality, even the reality of ours and other people's so-called mistakes, including relationship mistakes, in a non-judgemental way.

The evidence

As seen in the meta-analysis study conducted in over 24 schools mentioned above, mindfulness improves children's and teenagers' relationships by helping with:

- social skills
- positive relationship forming
- problems with interpersonal relationships.

TAKE-HOME AND TAKE-TO-SCHOOL MINDFUL RELATIONSHIPS TIPS

Mindfulness helps people connect deeply with others by enabling them to connect deeply with themselves. This means being fully aware and fully accepting of the here-and-now reality of who they are and what they are whole-heartedly able to share with other people. The great barrier to successful relationships is our focus on thoughts that are not grounded in our reality (such as past and future moments), including our thoughts about ourselves and other people. Mindfulness can be our great get-out-of-mind-jail-free opportunity.

- Don't think too much or too long about how you can help young people develop good life relationships. Just encourage, inspire and allow them to do this themselves, by helping them fully connect with their own and other people's hearts.
- Relate to your children in the way that you would like them to relate to other people.
- Be the change you want to see in the world! (Attributed to Mahatma Gandhi.)

Creativity

Being creative means being able to discover or uncover new and wonderful things about our world and ourselves. It means we are capable of looking at things differently, and therefore creating new ways of experiencing life. Being creative means being able to generate great life opportunities, now. Being creative helps us fully express who we really are, which leads to the development of our full potential in all aspects of our lives. How then can we help our children be more creative?

As mentioned previously, children and teens experience a desire to conform, to be like their peers, to be part of a tribe. They also feel forced to confirm to what society, their parents and their local environment expects of them. These forces to conform can act as an impediment to natural creativity. Fortunately, there are also forces that help teens to counter their need to conform and allow for opportunities to create.

Psychology defines creativity as a form of intelligence. There are two types: convergent intelligence, which allows us to focus on a single answer; and divergent intelligence, which allows us to have many answers. Convergent intelligence is often restrictive while divergent is creative and expansive. A classic test of divergent intelligence is the following sentence: 'How many uses can you think of for a brick?' Why don't you try this test yourself?

Both forms of thinking are crucial to encourage young people to step towards embracing acts of creativity and exploring ideas and situations within or even outside of their tribes.

Mindfulness can not only help children be creative, it can help them create great life opportunities — to shine their life light — on all of their life paths.

The challenge

We are living in a world that greatly values freedom — the freedom to think and act in the same way everyone else thinks and acts! This includes the freedom to be politically correct, and the freedom to conform to the will of most people, or the loudest, or the most influential. Political and social orthodoxy isn't new. Ever since humans formed tribes, we have had outsiders, and have been aware of the special difficulties and also opportunities of being an outsider. In 1953, the great American playwright Arthur Miller wrote a play called *The Crucible* about the Salem witch hunts of the seventeenth century. This was really a parable about the communist witch hunts in America in the late 1940s and early 1950s led by Senator Joseph McCarthy. 'Group think' has always been a significant problem, mainly because groups of people can think irrationally and destructively. We can do things in the apparent anonymity and lack of personal responsibility of a pack that we would never do as individuals. How, why and when do we stop being *'one'* and start being *'one of'*? How, why and when do we create limitations rather than opportunities?

Children are naturally creative. To see a young child play with a doll, for example, can be to see a great creative play because the doll can be absolutely real to that child; through their imagination they can create life. When children pass into the teen stage, they are often extremely conformist. Extreme conformity could be seen as radical non-creativity. It can lead to children exchanging their natural ability to create new experiences for a not-so-natural ability to just do what everyone else is doing, or what they did yesterday, or what people expect them to do.

The results of children losing too much of their natural

creativity and/or leaning too heavily into conformity can lead both individual and whole groups being tyrannized, feeling that they have to think and act like everyone. Lack of creativity also leads to a lack of realization of life opportunities, including recognizing and being our true selves. In the language of the psychologist Abraham Maslow, this means being self-actualized. In the language of the philosopher Socrates, this means to 'know thyself', i.e. discovering and therefore creating the best and fairest person that we can be. In any language this means being truly happy, fulfilled and free.

The solution

We all have opportunities to create alternative ways of thinking, to conduct living experiments, to be fully free of whatever it is that has stopped us from creating real-life possibilities. Mindfulness can really help young people develop, or remember, the experience of creativity and its benefits. Mindfulness can help young people discover, or rediscover, the freedom of just being, of experiencing life as a play rather than as a job, as infinite potential rather than as a list of limitations. Being creative by challenging orthodoxies or habitual ways of doing things can mean risking negative judgements and exclusion. It's vital for young people to be encouraged to have the resilience and fortitude to weather any such judgements and focus on the life opportunities instead.

The evidence

There is sound and growing scientific research evidence that supports the benefits of mindfulness for helping young people develop creative thinking. For example, a meta-analysis conducted in 2016 showed that there was an overall positive correlation between mindfulness and creativity.[4] Possible reasons for this connection include mindfulness being associated with a wide range of abilities and characteristics which help people be creative, including:

- an increased ability to switch perspectives[5]
- an increased ability to respond in a non-habitual fashion[6]
- a reduction in people's fear of judgement.[7]

Mindfulness helps expand young people's non-judgmental awareness, helping them to return to the natural state that they might have lost through social or anti-social conditioning, or mass expectations that can limit our ideas of who we are and what we can do. This can help young people be comfortable with uncertainty, which can valuably reduce their stress, as well as increase their creativity. Mindfulness does this by helping young people go beyond their mind-made habitual comfort or discomfort zones. A systematic review of research studies on the relationship between mindfulness and creativity showed that it's vital that young people's home and school environments fully allow their creative development, including reducing their judgment-related fear or anxiety, as well as their experience of uncertainty.[8]

There is also scientific research evidence that shows mindfulness training can help people, including young people, be more creative and therefore achieve the life benefits of being more creative. For example, a study conducted in 2012 showed that mindfulness improves divergent and also convergent thinking ability.[9]

TAKE-HOME AND TAKE-TO-SCHOOL MINDFUL CREATIVITY TIPS

An important take-home and take-to-school mindful well-being creativity message is that young people are naturally creative, and therefore naturally mindful. We don't need to teach creativity: all we need to do is create conditions that allow creativity to flourish, naturally.

- Encourage the act of creation by discovering and creating great life stories, activities and opportunities.
- Reveal to young people how you can create a happy ending no matter what your life story is or isn't.

PART 3

Strategies for mindful parenting

CHAPTER 6

Strategy 1:
Finding your calm

Angela North

Play therapy provides a method for raising a child's awareness of their inner world. From this self-awareness, many life skills are born.

What we can learn from play therapy

Mindfulness can be taught in many ways — and one of the best ways is through the language that all children speak: the language of play.

The domestic rat is one of the most playful creatures on earth. Plunk two little rats together and it's almost impossible to stop them whooping it up. Let them play for an hour a day or more and they will develop into chill dudes. But thwart a young rat's play, by rearing it alone for example, and you create an adult that loses its cool in social situations. When faced with opportunities to socialise, play-deprived rats will succumb to rat-rage, or run to a corner, quaking. Rats need play to cope with life. There is ample evidence that humans behave in the same way.[1]

Like rats, other primates — even fish! — children have a deeply embedded biological need for play. Play serves many purposes. 'Play fighting' activates the same brain chemicals as the fear we feel when we are genuinely threatened. In play, children deliberately trigger 'fight or flight' responses, such as in games of battle, tag or hide and seek, learning to tolerate stress in a safe environment.[2] They must also negotiate ad hoc rules with friends and find solutions to problems that arise — a creative endeavour that enhances their ability to learn. In other words, just like young rats, 'whooping it up' play helps us cope better with stress, practise solving problems, manage frustration and be more cooperative with others.

Footnote:

Play therapy provides an evidence-based method for raising the child's awareness of their own internal world. Influenced by the person-centred approach of Carl Rogers, non-directive play therapy (NDPT) is a particular approach developed by Virginia Axline. NDPT focuses on the child's moment-to-moment experience, with therapeutic responses that provide non-judgemental acceptance. The child hears their actions, struggles, wishes and desires reflected back to them while they play. The absence of judgement means the child is not distracted by anger or defensiveness, freeing them to focus on this growing self-awareness. Rather than impulsive reactions based on a confusion of feelings, the child begins to develop a more thoughtful (mindful) approach to their circumstances.

The fact that play is so necessary for development, and so inherently therapeutic, is something that play therapists around the globe have leveraged for decades. They take this already beneficial activity and enhance it, using mindful responses.

Play therapists closely observe a child at play, entering the rich world of the child's inner life. Here, battles are fought, justice is meted out (sometimes fairly, sometimes not), and characters are enlisted as needed. Play is not always for the faint-hearted: in the world of the imagination, children are free from judgement and discipline. Here, it can be safe to express their true feelings and wishes. For example, a child might feel powerless to prevent the arrival of a new sibling (such competition, such betrayal!). In play however, the 'baby doll' can be discarded, fed poison, sent to prison, or disappeared with a magic wand.

You might be alarmed by this behaviour, but as every play therapist will tell you, it is a normal, healthy way for children to let off steam, and helps them cope better with reality. In fact, adults do something similar, although it's less obvious to the observer. The next time you find yourself imagining a sudden, tragic ending to the driver who just cut you off, remember that this mental 'dark humour' is simply another way of using your imagination to cope.

In this chapter, you will discover many of the ways in which play therapists apply mindfulness. Some of these skills are deceptively simple: all of them can have a profound and far-reaching impact on your relationship with your child, and their ability to thrive. In the following chapter, you will have the additional option to apply these skills during special, therapeutic play sessions at home with your own child.

Staying calm

While the sight of a toddler having a tantrum on the floor of a supermarket is hardly new, the same behaviour from an adult would indeed be a surprise! Perhaps the biggest task of childhood is to master *emotion regulation,* so that as adults, we don't find ourselves collapsing in a heap when our favourite biscuits are out of stock. Emotion regulation — the ability to handle big feelings in healthy ways — is the foundation of resilience. When we gain this hard-earned skill, we bounce back quickly from setbacks. It takes most of childhood to learn, and for various reasons, not all adults achieve this milestone. They may not have supermarket meltdowns (although some do), but they might find themselves overreacting to small frustrations, becoming easily despondent or lashing out at others. Resilience offers us better mental health, better relationships with others, and better self-esteem — because knowing we can cope well when things get tough can feel like a superpower to be proud of.

Learning emotion regulation is not about repressing or ignoring our emotions. Try the following exercise and you will quickly see why.

Picture a pink elephant. Is it large or small? Is the pink a soft pastel, or a bright colour?

What is the elephant doing?

Now that you have imagined your elephant, spend the next minute thinking of something else.

Whatever you do, do not think about the pink elephant.

In reality, our mind struggles to supress thoughts — even those as ridiculous and unimportant as a pink elephant. It doesn't take long for the pink elephant to pop up, no matter how hard we try. In fact, trying to supress a thought will usually make it bigger and more intrusive. This is known as the Pink Elephant Paradox, and it is true for feelings too.

Many parents teach their children to repress or ignore feelings, in the belief that this will encourage more socially appropriate behaviours. While it might work — for a while — it can also backfire, increasing rather than decreasing problematic behaviours. But, like holding a ball full of air under water (or blocking a pink elephant from our thoughts), the moment a child is distracted or vulnerable, up pops the emotion — bigger than ever. If a child becomes especially good at repression, they may later find themselves experiencing high levels of anxiety, depression or other mental health issues. This can be bewildering, especially if there is no conscious awareness of the emotion's existence, such was the 'success' of a repression strategy.

The alternative is to practise acceptance and compassion in the face of emotions — both our own and our children's. If we are calm in the face of our own small frustrations and disappointments, our child learns an important message: *there is nothing to be afraid of here.* If we can remain calm and empathic when our child is in emotional turmoil, an additional message is communicated: a*ll emotions are a universal human experience, and you are safe to experience them, without judgement or shame.* Perhaps most important of all, your calm response frees your child to focus on the task of regaining their composure (practising emotional regulation), rather than being distracted by *your* big reactions.

Staying calm in the face of your children's emotions builds trust. And this trust will make navigating many aspects of parenting so much easier: more respectful collaboration, less angry opposition. The thermostat is a useful metaphor for the first step in mindful parenting: learning to respond, not react.

Thermostats vs thermometers

A thermometer is used to measure the temperature of a person, a room or the outside air. When the environment is hot, the thermometer goes up. We often react quickly to our children's rollercoaster of emotions in the same way. For example, when they become angry, we heat up quickly too. We are not at our best in these moments — a little like a child ourselves. This means when our children or teenagers are at their most distressed, there are two 'children' in the room, both having a meltdown, with nobody to model a calm response.

The occasional 'parent meltdown' is almost guaranteed. After all, parents are wonderfully complex, with their own histories, life challenges and day-to-day frustrations, like every other human. In fact, if parents were always calm, how would their children learn to cope with the emotional ups and downs of others? And would these same children feel like failures every time they got angry, or cried, or experienced other messy emotions?

We want children to be fully human, which means being unafraid of emotions, and with a growing ability to express them in healthy ways. This is the foundation of resilience, and it takes a lot of trial and error. We are not trying to create robots. The answer lies, as it often does, in balance. A parent's ability to respond calmly — *much* of the time — is sufficient for a child to learn that emotions are nothing to fear. In fact, when we remain calm, we can help children shift from a common belief that there are 'good' and 'bad' emotions, to an understanding that emotions are helpful signals, alerting us to a need — for comfort, honesty, even for food and rest! And for those other times, when we lose our cool? These are great opportunities to model accountability, by apologising, acknowledging what has happened, verbalising how we will handle it differently next time, and genuinely committing to that change.

So how do we achieve such a lofty goal as 'balance', when we may not have witnessed calm responses in our own childhood?

A thermostat works differently to a thermometer. It is designed to switch off when the environment gets too warm, only switching on again when things have returned to a normal baseline. It keeps the environment in an ideal 'sweet spot'. Mindfulness encourages us to act like a thermostat — lowering our own emotional reactions when our children are distressed. If responding calmly is not your natural style (and this is most of us), then practice is key to progress. Your child will need most or all their childhood to develop emotional regulation — so you won't be short of opportunities!

Practice makes progress: how to find your calm

Developing your ability to stay calm begins — always — with

self-compassion. Here are a few tips to begin building an inner reserve of calm for when you need it most.

Pay attention to your automatic reactions

Perhaps you feel tightness in your body or notice that your thoughts have started to speed up. Your inner talk might be angry or fearful. Often, you will find these thoughts are stuck in the past ('I can't believe they said that!') or worry for the future ('they'll never get a job if they don't work harder at school').

Be compassionate towards yourself

Take a moment to acknowledge the thoughts and feelings. It can help to name them, in a way that creates space between yourself and the thoughts, for example, 'That's my mind, getting stuck in the past' or 'There's my mind, imagining fearful things about the future'. You might choose an action that represents compassion towards yourself, such as placing your hand on your heart. Then set aside your thoughts, allowing them to be there, but not to dominate your focus. They are the mind's busy distraction from what is unfolding before you, and if they're important, they'll still be there when you return to them.

Return to the here and now

If you are struggling to stay present, wriggle your toes. You can do this even while listening to your child. Take one or two deep breaths, slowly, feeling your lungs expand then deflate. It might help to consider the following, particularly if you tend to rush in and problem solve:

> There is nothing I need to do here. I can simply be. I don't need to find answers, or to fix this. I can listen mindfully. I am curious to see what arises.

Now you are ready to lean into the exchange with your child, with mindfulness and curiosity.

Observe your child

Notice the early signs of frustration or distress. For young children, it might be irritability, a particular body language, or increasing acts of opposition. For older children, it might be silence, surliness, refusal to do a chore, or the timeless classic: an eye roll. This is your opportunity to respond, rather than react. Practise a specific response to these early signs that lead you to soften your body, quieten your mind and let your emotional thermostat switch off.

Troubleshooting

While practice leads to progress, things don't always go to plan. Here are a few common issues you may encounter, and how you might address them.

Taboo emotions

Taboo emotions are those that your upbringing, culture, spiritual beliefs and life experiences may have encouraged you to avoid, because they are considered harmful or shameful. Taboos make it difficult to remain calm when your child is expressing those emotions. However, emotions are not the problem. We connect emotions to poor behaviours and give them a bad rap. But emotions are simply messages from all our senses, alerting us to information about ourselves and our environment. And there are as many good acts that can be inspired by so-called 'bad' emotions, as there are bad acts. Here are some examples:

- Anger inspires a girl to step in and protect a child being bullied.
- Fear motivates a group of children to form a climate change action group.
- Jealousy helps a shy teenager recognize his own desire for financial independence, leading him to find the courage to get a part-time job.

It is time to farewell the idea of good and bad emotions. What we (and our children) *do* with those emotions — how we act on them — is a separate issue. Remember: discouraging a child from feeling a particular emotion (even in a subtle way like calling anger a softer word such as 'mad' or 'annoyed') will only increase its force. Resistance breeds persistence. Emotions are there to gain our attention, and they have a way of getting louder until they succeed.

You might like to spend some time thinking about your own childhood, and how each emotion was treated. If you were proud of an achievement but were told to stop 'showing off', perhaps you consider pride something to be hidden, for fear of judgement. You might not cope well when your child shows pride — you might even find yourself calling *them* a show-off. There are many ways that we can subtly train children to ignore or repress their feelings. The more you can accept your own emotions — all of them — the more you can teach your child to accept theirs. Paradoxically, the more we accept our emotions as they arise, the greater control we have over our behaviours. This is true for adults and children alike.

Ghosts in the nursery

Everybody brings a history of their *own* childhood to their role of parent. If you struggle to remain calm in the face of particular emotions, you will have a clue about which emotions were 'taboo' in your childhood. Likewise, your inner calm may escape you in the face of certain behaviours, based on what you were taught about intelligence, creativity, productivity, gender roles, sexuality, religion and duty to family.

If you reflect on your own childhood, you may be able to articulate some of these rules and beliefs. Other rules will be more subtle, there but never verbalized. All will significantly influence your thoughts about your own child, and the emotions that arise in you when they struggle. If you felt loved because of your academic success, how do you respond when your child struggles in school? If you were raised to conform to strict roles about gender, what do you say when your pre-school son wants to wear a fairy costume? These are the 'ghosts in the nursery', a metaphor introduced by social worker and psychoanalyst Selma Fraiberg to describe the relationship between a parent's early experiences of how they were raised, and their own parenting style. As Fraiberg says: 'In every nursery there are ghosts. They are the visitors from the unremembered past of the parents.'[3]

When we understand the experiences that influenced us, we can begin to honour those messages that continue to be helpful and let go of those that are not. If you are not sure where to begin, ask yourself: how much of yourself do you accept wholeheartedly and without reservation? What parts of yourself would you rather others did not see? These are clues to the rejected parts of ourselves that we forced into the shadows. This might have been a useful strategy while growing up — we all want love and approval after all. But does it serve you now? Does it serve your child?

To a large degree, our expression of who we are is directed by the culture we grew up in. We may not *want* to change this outward self, nor reject the values that stem from that culture. But our internal world is entirely ours, and we are free to observe our thoughts, notice long-held judgements, and play with ideas of acceptance and kindness. Here, parenting our children becomes about choice, rather than reactions. When we leave our internal world unexamined, the judgements that live there have a habit of haunting us, and our children. Even relatively benign comments from others can stick like glue. As one mother shared during a parenting course:

> I remember my mum once said, 'You never finish anything.' She was annoyed because I wanted to give up learning tennis. Years later, I felt like I hadn't made it career-wise, and I found myself thinking, *it's my fault; I never finish anything*. In reality, I have a degree, good relationships and a reasonable income. But that idea kept haunting me. Now I find I can't

> stand it if my kids give up on anything. It's like my biggest goal, for them to be persistent and never give up. I get angry and have to walk away — but then I feel bad, because they're only in primary school.

Our child, our mirror

Not only might you find your own childhood hijacking your ability to remain calm, but many parents report finding a particular age more challenging than other ages. If we had a difficult, even traumatic period in our own lives, chances are that when our child reaches the same age, we might struggle.

This is a phenomenon often seen in families, made worse because nobody is aware that it is happening. Our children act like a mirror to our own childhood upheavals. If you were four when your parents separated, you may feel overly protective when your own child turns four. If you experienced a traumatic event when you were seven, you may experience an unnamed anxiety when your child is the same age. If you felt unsafe as a teenager, you may struggle to allow your own teen to take age-appropriate risks, leading to arguments and rebellion.

It helps to reflect on the big events of your own life, acknowledge how old you were, and be mindful that when your child is that age, memories may be triggered. Mindful awareness can alert you to your own need for soothing and compassion, so that you do not parent from fear or anger that belongs in the past.

Struggling to find the words

If the benefits of remaining calm make sense to you, but the ability still eludes you at times, it may help to continue your practice — without words. This removes one of the elements — the one that requires the most amount of thinking. Chances are, when you are getting annoyed or worried, your 'fight or flight' instincts have already kicked in, which makes thinking harder. This is especially likely when both we and our children are tired — everybody is close to a meltdown. So rather than 'forcing' calm, let go of the words and try simply *acting* with compassion instead. Grab a blanket and wrap it around your upset toddler. Give them a hug and a sippy cup (the act of sucking through a straw can help with sensory calming). Create a cosy cubby (under a table, in a cupboard — anywhere 'cave-like'), using pillows and soft toys, for a young child on the verge of a meltdown. Then leave them to it. Make a hot chocolate or a snack for an angry teen, then hand them the TV remote and sit together for a while (if you're able). Words are not always necessary to show empathy and the physical movement will help calm your own nervous system.

CHAPTER 7

Strategy 2: Empathic reflections

Angela North

Who am I?

In the beginning, we are who our parents think we are. Through infancy and the early years, we do not yet have a solid, cohesive picture of ourselves. Our parents' words and actions help us build that picture. So the development of our sense of *self* — our picture of who we are — occurs first through the eyes of our parents. The parent whose face lights up when we enter the room tells us we are loved and valued. The parent who firmly sets boundaries, without anger or resentment, tells us they will keep us safe until we can do it for ourselves. The parent who listens to us, showing compassion and interest, helps us feel seen, heard and understood. All of these messages will eventually become our internal voice and, as we discussed earlier in this book, we want that voice to sound like a life coach — always steering us to be our best, compassionate and most confident selves.

So how can we ensure that we are building a life coach in our children?

Building an inner life coach

A positive inner voice first develops from parents' positive responses. Ideally, these will encourage the child to tune inwards, using the power of compassion to calm down. Empathic reflections begin with acts of mindfulness, such as drawing your child's attention to the present moment, labelling their feelings, wishes or wants, and communicating acceptance. Regardless of the emotion or behaviour, your message is 'I see you, I understand, and I care'. Empathic reflections are a powerful tool, impacting on children's wellbeing even before they have learned spoken language.

A baby cries, and her father responds 'Oooh, what's the matter little one? Daddy's here. Let's see if your feet are cold.' The words are meaningless to her, but the tone and gentle hug are not. She is already learning that she is valued, that she will be comforted when upset, and that her needs will be met. Her father is matching his tone and touch to her own emotions, an infant-friendly, non-verbal version of 'empathic reflections'.

Just as the father did for his infant daughter, you can observe your child — their words and actions — and reflect your understanding of what you see. Your tone is empathic — not because you necessarily approve of the behaviour, but because in this moment, you understand that your child is wrestling with self-control.

It's important to understand that empathy is not the same as agreement. It simply demonstrates a deeper understanding of the need behind the behaviour, and that compassion will decrease problematic behaviours faster than criticism will.

PRACTICE MAKES PROGRESS
REFLECTING WHAT YOU SEE: NAME THE FEELING, WISH OR WANT

When you see your child showing a particular emotion, label it and acknowledge the feeling, wish or want using an empathic tone. Ensure that your tone and facial expression reflect the delight, sadness, or urgency they are communicating. Use your body language to show that you are focused and paying attention. Empathic reflections are helpful for *all* emotions — because we want children to be aware of the full range of their emotional experience. Some examples are below:

- You're happy to see Grandma!
- You're sad that you can't play with Sam today.
- You are really angry at Mummy right now.
- You love bath time — baths make you so happy.

Every time you empathically reflect your child's experience, you are giving them a developmental gift-bag of goodies. Naming their emotions helps children develop a vocabulary that will enable better communication. Children who can't tell you how they feel can experience higher levels of frustration and behavioural problems. In fact, this ability to recognise our own (and others') emotions is a foundation of emotional intelligence, which is found to be equally or more important to life success than IQ.[1]

Your empathy is also critical — we all calm down at a faster rate when we experience empathy. Judgement, on the other hand, tends to make us feel defensive, and distracts from the calming process. If you want to drag a meltdown out, offer judgement. If you want the quickest recovery possible, try empathy.

Hana is four years old. She is crying loudly, a nightly ritual her mother Jasmine has come to expect, because Hana hates brushing her teeth and protests every time. Jasmine tries to cajole Hana, praising her for being a 'big girl' and offering the well-worn bribe of an extra story at bedtime. It doesn't work, and neither does a lecture on dental health, or the threat of no bedtime story. Hana simply gets louder.

Why Jasmine's approach didn't work: Roadblocks to open communication

The most common ways of responding to children are not necessarily problematic in the general course of the day. But if your aim is to build a child's self-awareness, empathy, resilience, and a close, respectful relationship, then your typical communication might represent a 'roadblock'. Roadblocks prevent or block open communication about feelings, wishes and wants. They cause a reaction in the listener, child or adult that leads them to feel defensive, frustrated or dismissed. Examples of roadblocks include:

- giving orders
- asking questions
- warning
- moralizing
- offering solutions
- giving facts
- criticizing
- praising.

In fact, a child's life is filled with these communications, from morning until bedtime. They may result in obedience, with some children, at least some of the time. And at other times, you will be too busy or fatigued to do anything else. But with each interaction, there is an opportunity to learn more about your child and teach more than simply how to follow orders.

Roadblocks versus empathic reflections

Jasmine has been practising empathic reflections with her daughter, Hana. She still feels a little clumsy with it and has to remember to use a calm, empathic voice. But she is getting quicker at noticing the 'feeling, wish or want' that Hana is expressing.

Today, when Hana frowns at the mention of teeth-brushing time, Jasmine states, 'You *really* don't like brushing your teeth.' Hana stops, surprised by the empathy.

'I HATE it!' she declares, using a word that is usually admonished.

'You wish you *never* had to do it,' responds Jasmine.

'Never, ever, ever, ever!!' says Hana. She finds several more ways of expressing her dislike, and each is met with calm acknowledgement and empathy.

Jasmine notices that Hana's body language has relaxed, and that she is allowing her mother to put toothpaste on the brush while they talk. Jasmine takes a chance, and says, 'You know, I don't like it either. It's SO boring!' She rolls her eyes comically, and Hana laughs. In a time far shorter than a tantrum would take, Hana and Jasmine have discovered something: when we are heard and understood, we feel better, and can sometimes do the most unpleasant (but necessary) things.

Acknowledging Hana's feelings and her wish to avoid brushing her teeth has achieved more than just dental hygiene. Empathic reflections have many positive outcomes, including:

Calming down, building resilience

Repeated use of empathic reflections gives multiple opportunities to shift from distress to calm. Over time, your child will rely less and less on you to calm down, as the experience becomes their 'inner voice'. This skill has the added bonus of contributing to self-esteem, allowing your child to add 'I can do feelings' to their sense of self.

Improving the likelihood of compliance

When a child feels judged, they will tend to resist limits and boundaries as a way of 'saving face' and communication between parent and child can easily become a power battle. In contrast, when a child feels understood and accepted, they have no need to 'save face', and resistance lowers. If your child is being oppositional, and empathic reflections help them (eventually!) to comply, resist the urge to follow up with any version of 'I told you so'. You may think it, because you have the wisdom that life experience has provided. But a smug or knowing response to compliance is shaming the very behaviour you wanted to encourage. Guess what will happen next time?

If a child is drowning, it's not the time to teach them to swim: The importance of timing

We all want our children to benefit from our hard-won wisdom and to share our values. This is why we communicate our thoughts, ideas and solutions when it seems relevant. Empathic reflections are not intended to replace our wisdom. *It is all about timing.* When a child is overwhelmed by big emotions, the 'thinking' part of their brain has temporarily shut down, a neuro-chemical response to stress that means they cannot focus on our words. Ever noticed your child gets louder and angrier when you try to 'calm them down' with practical advice? Your advice might be valuable, but not during an emotional storm. Use empathic reflections to help your child feel understood and save your wisdom for later.

Building emotional intelligence

Words have power. When we speak to our children, our words can either forge strong relationships, or erode them. As Gary Chapman, author of *Love as a Way of Life,* so eloquently states, 'our words can be bullets or seeds'.[2] Every time a child's feeling, wish or want is reflected to them, they connect your words to the inner experience of their body. Their ability to express themselves becomes both broader and more accurate. Twentieth-century philosopher Ludwig Wittgenstein was quoted as saying 'the limits of my language are the limits of my world.' A child (or adult) who cannot accurately communicate their inner world to others is limited, frustrated, and will have difficulty navigating relationships. Empathic reflections are the seeds of self-awareness, offering the language of emotions and the pathway to connection.

The green-eyed monster is ... all of us

Anja has a new baby brother. She's not very keen on the arrival. Her mother scolds her, telling her she should love her baby brother. Anja has nowhere to put her confusion of feelings, and now understands that these feelings are bad — that she is bad.

The alternative? Anja's mother acknowledges Anja's ambivalence, recognizes and names her jealousy as a normal, human emotion. She says something like:

> 'You feel a bit jealous about your new brother.
> Mum and Dad love you very much, and we
> always will. But I understand — it will take a
> little while for you to get used to sharing us.'

Anger is just another emotion

Mahia is five and, after a big day at school, is having a meltdown. She yells, 'I hate you!' to her mother. Her mother spanks her, saying Mahia is never to say that again.

Mahia is learning that anger is very, very bad.

The alternative? Mahia's mother recognizes the underlying fatigue, and that Mahia likely needs rest, perhaps food and water. She responds calmly, saying:

> 'You want me to know you are angry. And tired too. I'm going to get a snack for you. Why don't you snuggle on the couch if you want to.'

Joy – only for toddlers?

Six-year-old Samantha is laughing and giggling loudly with a friend, pulling faces. Her father tells her to stop being silly. She feels embarrassed in front of her friend.

The alternative? Samantha's father removes the criticism and provides a model of self-care and accountability for meeting his own needs. He says:

> 'You have so much fun when you get together — I love that! I'm feeling a bit tired and grumpy though — would you mind helping me by taking your fun to the backyard?'

Self-care: Noticing what makes us happy

Avery has had a tough day at school and tells her mum she is having a bath. Later, Avery is calmer and more talkative. Her mum sees the bathroom – candles, body scrub, soap bubbles and a towel on the floor. Frustrated, she says, 'For goodness sakes, Avery, come and clean up this mess. I'm sick and tired of picking up after you.' The happy mood evaporates.

The alternative? Avery's mum helps her recognize her developing 'emotion regulation' skills — making a self-care choice that clearly worked. She also establishes a boundary around cleaning up, remaining calm and empathic. The good mood — and their relationship — is preserved. She says:

> 'Hey, well done — you have discovered you are a "bath" girl!' I'm glad it made a difference sweetheart — always good to know what works for us when we've had a tough day.' (Offers hug.) 'You need to put all your bath stuff away, too. Put it all in the top drawer for next time.'

The rollercoaster of friendships

Malik and his best friend Henry went to kindergarten together, and now they go to the same school. They play ball every lunchtime. 'Two peas in a pod,' their mothers say. Today, Malik comes home angry. According to Malik, Henry ran off to play with a new student, leaving Henry to spend his lunchtime alone. Hearing this, his mum feels angry at Henry's insensitivity, and says, 'I don't want you to play with him again! This isn't the first time he's been a bad friend.'

The next day, Henry and Malik play ball again, and the new student joins them too. Malik doesn't tell his mum. Her judgement and directive lead Malik to think she might get angry at him.

The alternative? Malik's mum can acknowledge his feelings and, if it is relevant, help Malik understand Henry's behaviour in a context that is less personal and hurtful. Then she can encourage Malik to practise his own growing ability to problem solve. She says:

> 'Sounds like you felt pretty sad when you couldn't find Henry. And perhaps a bit jealous, too, that he and the new boy got to play together. I guess Henry is still learning how to be a friend, especially when he has *two* friends

that he wants to play with.' (Malik's mum hugs him and waits for him to settle.) 'I wonder how you'd like to handle this when you see Henry tomorrow.'

The amazing human ability to feel opposite emotions, at the same time

Levi's costume is laid out next to his bed, ready for the following morning when he will lead the Book Week Parade at school. His dad is reading a bedtime story when Levi starts to cry, saying, 'I don't want to do the parade.' Levi's dad hugs him, telling him he will be okay, there is nothing to be worried about. Levi cries even harder.

The alternative? Levi's dad can reflect what Levi is feeling, and also help Levi understand that sometimes we feel two opposite feelings at the same time. Levi had been excited all week — about his costume and the honour of leading the march. Levi's dad says:

'Sounds like you're feeling a bit nervous about tomorrow.' (Levi's dad hugs him and waits for him to settle.) 'I remember how excited you were to be chosen. I wonder how it would feel if you didn't do it. Perhaps you're feeling a bit nervous AND a bit excited — all mixed up together.'

A place for sadness

Jane and her dad are driving to her mum's house. Jane is fourteen and has just seen her friends on social media, hanging out without her. Her dad asks her why she's 'glum' and, in a rare moment of honesty, she says she feels depressed. He says, 'Don't be ridiculous, you're fourteen! What have you got to be depressed about?' Jane has no idea how to answer that and becomes even more silent and withdrawn.

The alternative? Jane's father can reflect her feelings with empathy and see if she is ready to say more.

'It sounds like you're going through a tough time, love.' (Jane's dad might then wait and see what Jane tells him in this space of quiet empathy.) Even if she remains silent, he can still use empathic reflections simply by saying, 'It must be hard to put what you're feeling into words.' He could also park the car and give Jane his full attention, but for many teenagers, such eye-to-eye contact can be a little overwhelming, which is why the best conversations often happen when you are together but focusing on an activity such as cooking, driving or walking.

Children feel grief, too

Theo is nine years old. His grandfather has died, and he is at a large wake with all his family. Theo's aunt tells him, 'Don't cry, or you'll make your mother sad.'

The alternative? Theo's aunt gives him a hug, acknowledges his feelings and reminds him that he has the support and understanding of his whole family:

> 'You're feeling sad, I know you love your grandpa very much. You are not alone. We all love him, we are all sad, and we will all feel our love for grandpa, together. You can come and ask for a hug, or to talk about Grandpa, whenever you want to.'

Building a close relationship

Many parents experience high levels of stress attending to busy lives. It is easy for parenting to feel like a daily chore rather than a process of discovery. Without mindfulness, there may be fewer moments of spontaneous joy, deep connection or a sense of wonder. In practising empathic reflections, we stop asking questions, offering solutions or any of the other things we ordinarily do. These things come from our mind. Instead, we approach our child with open curiosity, ready to tune into *their* mind, *their* experience. Attunement brings great gifts, with a deeper aware-ness of the child's likes, dislikes, fears and wishes. The more you do it, the more your child will reveal of their self, as they build trust in the space you are creating.

Safety

Children are constantly making sense of their world, but they have a brain which is still developing and limited life experience to assist. This occasionally leads to some weird and wonderful conclusions.

> A four-year-old was going on a holiday, and while she had previously been to the airport to farewell family, watching until the plane was just a tiny speck in the sky, she had never been on a plane herself. She was very excited. Once the plane was airborne, she turned to her mother and asked, 'When do we start getting smaller?'[3]

> A five-year-old spent his birthday at the museum with family. He particularly loved the display that showed the evolution of the human species. Later, he said to his dad, 'You know when I was a monkey in mummy's tummy?' His father, confused, asked him what he meant. 'Y'know — because we start as mon-keys and become people later on.'

Sometimes, the conclusions children come to are funny and make for great family stories. At other times, however, the conclusions are unhelpful, even harmful. Young children have yet to fully develop their understanding that others have thoughts and feelings that are separate from their own. This ego-centric thinking is a normal part of early development, but problematic if the child blames themselves for their parent's separation, for example. Empathic reflections allow a parent to follow their child's thinking — peeling away the layers — to reach their core beliefs. With every reflection, you may find the conversation goes deeper. This gives an opportunity to respond and, where necessary, comfort and reassure.

> **Rupert climbs into the car after school with a stormy face. Megan knows her son finds Grade 2 tiring, and especially today as it was the house swimming carnival. 'How was the swimming?' she asks, handing him a muesli bar. Rupert throws the snack on the floor, muttering, 'I HATE muesli bars.' Megan chooses to ignore the poor manners — she can address that later. She has been using empathic reflections for a while now. She knows the snack is not likely the problem and, ordinarily, Rupert is a well-mannered and empathic boy. She has learned that reflecting _Rupert's_ experience in this moment will be more helpful than telling him _her_ thoughts on the matter.**
>
> _Megan:_ **'Looks like you're sick of muesli bars.'**

Rupert: 'They're gross! And I'm HUNGRY!'
Megan: 'You're hungry, and now you're dis-
appointed all we have is a muesli bar.'
Rupert: ' … yeah. Can we make a banana
milkshake at home?'
Megan: 'Sure, we can do that.'
Rupert: 'I just wanna go home. School is
stupid.'
Megan: 'You've had enough today, huh?'
Rupert starts to cry. 'Mrs K was mean to me.
She told me off in front of the whole class,
just because I forgot my towel.'
Megan: 'Sounds like you felt kinda embar-
rassed, in front of your friends.'
Rupert: 'I'm just stupid!'

Rupert's cry turns into sobs. Megan reaches over
and gives him a hug. Now she knows what the
real issue is, she can comfort him while he releases the big emotions he has been holding on to all
day. She doesn't need to advise, teach, or organ-
ize a towel-remembering strategy — at least not
now. Sitting compassionately with Rupert while
his sobs turn to sniffles and his body returns to
calm is exactly what Rupert needs. Later, when
Rupert is calm and content, Megan will address
his misconception that forgetting a towel and
getting into trouble means that he is 'stupid'. She
might also gently remind him that next time he

**is feeling angry or sad, he can choose to ask for a
hug and get his needs met directly.**

Consider the 'roadblocks' to communication discussed earlier.
Megan had many options for responding to Rupert. She could
have asked questions, such as 'Why are you so grumpy?' She
could have given a warning: 'Watch those manners or you'll be in
time out.' Her roadblocks and judgements would have increased
Rupert's anger and distracted them both. Rupert might never
have uncovered the issue that was troubling him. Megan's willingness to follow his lead, listening without judgement, is what
unpeeled the layers and led to insight. This is especially important when we uncover a belief that is harmful. Empathic reflections are our pass to the inner workings of our children's minds.
Only when we know, can we help.

Rupert's upset may seem ordinary, and perhaps undeserving
of such patience and effort. However, he is learning that his mum
is a highly valued source of support — not just for everyday concerns, but for those usually hidden for fear of embarrassment,
shame or punishment. With empathic reflections, a channel of
communication is opened and will remain open throughout the
teenage years and beyond, offering a powerful safety net. This
child has a trusted sounding board to discuss everything from
social problems, first romantic feelings, worries about a friend,
decisions about sex, drugs and alcohol, and all the other challenges that must be navigated.

Empathic reflections are not a replacement for behavioural
boundaries. In fact, empathy and boundaries are both essential for healthy development. But when a child is experiencing

overwhelming emotions or resistance, both parent and child will benefit when understanding is prioritized, and consequences — where appropriate — come later.

Older children and teenagers – where trust takes time to build

Empathic reflections can profoundly impact relationships, even ones that have been fraught for years. If you recognize that your own struggle to stay calm and listen mindfully has impacted your relationship, building trust will take patience and time. In fact, a commitment to calm communication and empathic reflections may initially trigger even greater anger or withdrawal from your child. Psychologists call this 'testing for safety': past hurts, disappointments and experiences of shame are not easily forgotten, and your child will want to check if this new behaviour is a legitimate shift, or not to be trusted.

'When I was a teenager, my mum and I argued a lot. It got to the point where I never shared anything with her, and mostly avoided her. One day, she responded unexpectedly to my distress about breaking up with a boyfriend. She listened, and then she took me out for lunch to talk some more. She even let me have a cigarette, which completely blew my mind. I knew she wasn't saying 'now it's okay for you to smoke', but her actions showed, more than anything, that she knew I was wrestling with bigger issues at that moment. I have never forgotten it. Later, she did a course that taught meditation and mindful acceptance. At first, I thought it was a trick, or some 'woo woo' rubbish she was into. But it made a huge difference to our relationship — we became much closer, and I really respect the humility and effort it must have taken. It's a rare thing, to change like that.'

It helps to remember, as often as possible, to begin with compassion for yourself. It is difficult, but certainly not impossible, to learn something that we were not modelled as children ourselves. Like most things, it takes practice.

Each time your attempts at empathic reflections are rejected, remind yourself that this is one more opportunity to prove your commitment — that this is no 'flash in the pan' trick, but a new way of being. Rejection is not failure, but a step closer to trust. Your child may be rejecting your attempts, but they are also watching you closely, and hoping that this new way of communicating is here to stay. A gracious acceptance that your child is not yet willing to trust your empathy (rather than an angry or frustrated response) *is as important* as the empathic reflection itself, showing that you are being accountable for past behaviours.

Your child or teen doesn't want to trust too quickly, because the disappointment (if the trust was unfounded) would be overwhelming. And if you do trip up on this path to building trust, you might try saying something like the example below, using your own words. Because you can also be a beautiful model for accountability by saying sorry, and acknowledging that you are learning something new, which takes time.

> 'I've realized that my reactions to you in the past have meant that you have a hard time trusting me. It means you probably don't want to talk to me about important things or tell me what's going on in your life. That's the opposite of what I want for you — for us. I'm determined to get better at being calm, listening instead of talking, and understanding. I know it will take a while for you to trust me — please take as long as you need to. I want you to know that, with practice, I will get better at this. Because I love you very much, and you are worth it.'

CHAPTER 8

Strategy 3: Setting limits while protecting self-esteem

Angela North

Discussions about parenting are more prevalent now than in previous periods of history. As a result, many parents are aware that punitive styles of parenting (think 'my way or the highway' and 'because I said so!') do not often lead to good outcomes.

Punitive parenting and mental health

Children who are naturally easy going, passive or obedient may tolerate strict, controlling parenting for long periods — perhaps their entire childhood. However, their internal sense of self — including hopes, fears and goals — have a habit of wanting to be heard. And if these differ from a parent's hopes, fears and goals, a tension builds. This tension may turn inwards, so that the child (or perhaps they are now an adult) becomes depressed or anxious. They may develop addictions to keep the distress at bay. Or this tension may turn outwards, expressed as aggression, rebellion or even complete rejection of the parent–child relationship.

In either case, the child may experience an intolerable level of suppression, and this will affect their self-esteem and mental health. Our relationships with our parents are the first experiences of love that we have. They form a template for all later relationships. If the parent is overly controlling, the child learns not to trust their own intuition about themselves. They may conclude that they are not worthy of love for who they are, but rather only for what they give and do for others. This tension may be less if the child is raised in a collectivist culture, where the needs of the group are emphasized, and doing for others is highly regarded. However, all people need some freedom of expression, and families vary, regardless of culture, as to how much flexibility and acceptance of difference is allowed.

Building self-esteem: Let's be honest

So how do we discipline our children while still allowing space for them to feel heard and understood? How do we ensure that in setting behavioural limits, we continue to protect self-esteem?

The self-esteem movement of the 1980s attempted to answer that very question. In a well-meaning attempt to steer away from harsh authoritarian parenting, parents and educators were told to encourage their children's self-esteem by providing consistently positive praise. However, this social experiment did not create well-functioning adults with high self-esteem. Indeed, this approach has since been described as a 'quasi-religious con'.[1] A little harsh perhaps, but there is no doubt that this attempt to swing parenting culture from harsh to empathic swung a little too far.

Self-esteem is great, it seems, if it is based in *reality*.[2] Otherwise, we risk raising a generation of somewhat narcissistic individualists who expect praise for little effort, and find it hard to stay motivated without constant, external encouragement. Self-awareness is also sacrificed — personal shortcomings are glossed over or ignored, leaving little room for honest self-reflection and personal growth.

In the adult world, worthy achievements involve persistence through boredom and failure. Nobody will sit by your side offering you praise while you write a thesis, complete your fiftieth job application or finish the restoration of your dream car. Many of the goals that offer the highest rewards are achieved in relative isolation. If our persistence relies on the praise of others, we cannot sustain the effort required.

In addition to unwarranted praise, the self-esteem movement offered the motto 'everyone's a winner'. The reality is that oftentimes, we lose. If we have had no practice at tolerating that reality, life is going to disappoint us severely.

A full and honest appraisal

Given that the downsides of being a harsh, critical parent are self-evident and that well-meaning 'self-esteem boosting' praise may backfire, how might mindful parenting provide an alternative? We know our children begin to develop a sense of self from their earliest moments in life. We have a powerful opportunity to contribute to the picture they are forming. When we practise mindful parenting, we can assist our children to become *aware* of their true selves by offering a full and honest appraisal, equally inclusive of strengths and weaknesses, presented without judgement.

In this space, our child sees themselves clearly. They are free to unfurl their potential without the distorting effects of shame that judgement brings. It is the simple and powerful combination of *reality* and *compassion*. Here are some examples of possible scenarios and responses:

> *Ren:* 'It wasn't me who left the chocolate on the couch.'
> *Parent:* 'You'd like me to think it wasn't you. I know you're just learning to tell the truth. And you will feel SO proud of yourself when you do it. I'll help you by letting you know when I can see you're struggling.'

> *Caitlyn:* 'Oh no! I left my bag at Dad's house!'
> *Parent:* 'That's okay. You haven't learned the habit of using your checklist yet. Is there anything you can think of that might help?'
> *Caitlyn:* 'I suppose I could set an alarm on my phone for Thursday mornings to use the checklist?'

Parent: 'Great idea — give that a try.'

Kamala: 'Why didn't anyone pick me for their team?'

Parent: 'You'd like to be picked for the team, but I notice you don't spend a lot of time practising. If it's important to you to be picked, then you can choose to spend more time on it. If you can't really be bothered, then perhaps it's not really your thing.'

When behaviours require discipline: How to draw the line and still protect self-esteem

With the cultural swing away from punitive parenting, many parents found themselves at a loss for an alternative and found themselves avoiding discipline altogether.

For some parents who experienced highly critical, even abusive discipline, the act of setting limits may trigger memories and bodily responses (where we often store trauma). Even if you are not consciously aware of this, if you find yourself recognizing problematic behaviour, and not stepping in, it is important to take stock and ask yourself why. This self-reflection requires compassion and, sometimes, support from others.

The reality is that discipline is essential for our children's mental health and ability to thrive. When parents lean into the task with calm compassion, discipline teaches children:

- Empathy: recognizing the impact of their behaviours on others

- Emotion regulation: managing feelings in ways that support mental health
- Accountability: that we are responsible for our own choices
- Social skills: it's easier to connect with others when I am in control of my impulses
- Self-esteem: I learn to cope in healthy ways — my growing resilience feels good!

Practice makes progress

First: Calm the storm before asking for compliance

If you first acknowledge the feeling, wish or urge your child is experiencing, they are more likely to begin calming down. You are showing them that you understand their perspective, even though you cannot allow the behaviour. When children feel understood and accepted, they are far less defensive and resistant to our limits. So, begin with empathic reflections.

> **'You're angry at him for taking your toy.'**
> **'You wanted to draw on the wall.'**

Second: Keep your language impersonal

Parents will often set limits using personal language that has the sting of judgement. Phrases like 'you shouldn't do that!', 'what were you thinking?!' or 'don't let me see you do that again' all feel very targeted and critical. Yet it takes years of practice and brain development for children to manage their impulses and not act on them. Targeted criticisms while they are still learning are a little like saying 'how dare you be a child!' We want our expectations to match our child's age, stage of development and any life challenges they might be facing.

The alternative is the use of neutral language that communicates the limit, without inherent criticism. We are rejecting the behaviour — not the child. This is the key to making your limit setting a therapeutic process, because attacking the problematic behaviour, not the child, is what protects self-esteem.

The impersonal message also serves as a reminder that learning to managing impulses is a universal task that applies to all of us. When your child hears this message, they are no longer hearing judgement, but rather a shared 'we are all in this together'. No longer you versus me, but instead, a parent saying, 'I remember this. It's tough, isn't it? Don't worry, I'm here with you while you work it out, and regain self-control.' For example:

> **'One thing we can't do is hit people.**
> **You can hit this rubber toy.'**
> **'The walls are not for drawing on.**
> **Let's find some paper.'**

Third: Allow time for struggle

Maintaining a calm, matter-of-fact tone is an important part of the process. It allows your child time to calm down, raise objections and eventually accept the limit. The time it takes to calm down will decrease with age, and frequent use of this strategy will speed that learning up considerably. Simply continue to use empathic reflections while maintaining the limit you have set.

Sam: 'Mummy! Elijah hit me!'

Elijah: 'But he took my toy!'

Parent: 'You're angry with Sam for taking your toy.'

Elijah: 'He shouldn't do that!'

Parent: 'It made you really upset, because that's your special toy.'

Elijah: 'Yeah …'

Parent: 'You didn't want Sam to take your toy. One thing we can't do is hit people.'

Elijah: 'Well, he shouldn't take my toy.'

Parent: 'That's right, Sam should ask you first. I'll help Sam with that in a little while.

Elijah: 'He's a stupid-head.'

Parent: 'You're still angry at Sam.'

(silence)

Parent: 'You wish you could, but one thing we can't do is hit people.'

Elijah: '… sorry Mummy.'

(hugs)

Parent: 'After lunch, we can talk about what you can do when you get angry at Sam.'

If raising objections is a key resistance strategy for your child, they may have developed a habit of opposition. The saying 'any attention is good attention' might apply here. To change this pattern, we can meet the need for attention while encouraging different, healthier behaviours. We do this by withdrawing when the behaviours are argumentative, and providing a great deal of love, acceptance and empathy when the child has stopped.

A lack of judgement is critical here. Your child is not naughty; they are simply attempting to get a need for connection met. You might say:

> **'I'm finished talking about this. Sometimes it's hard to calm down. Let's go get a drink of water together, or you can come and find me when you're ready for a hug.'**

Remember, an empathic tone is critical to the success of this strategy, so that it feels like an opportunity to learn, rather than a personal judgement of your child.

Advanced limit setting: Highlighting choices for ultimate accountability

We all know adults who lack accountability for their behaviours. They might be consistently unreliable. Perhaps they make a lot of excuses or become highly defensive to avoid discussion about the impact of their behaviours. They may offer 'false' apologies — an apology with no commitment to change — so that the problematic behaviour continues. In adults, this tends to indicate an area of development that has not progressed, so that, with regards to accountability, they are more child than adult.

When we raise children, we can maximize the development of accountability. In the future, their relationships with partners, family, friends and colleagues benefit by their ability to self-reflect, own their mistakes and make genuine change where necessary.

As with many of the strategies described, this begins with empathic reflections, because empathy removes shame, which is a roadblock to open communication.

The second element is to focus on choices. Offering choices when a child is calming down can help speed up the process. It returns a sense of control to a child who is resisting feeling 'controlled'. It can be a great strategy for helping a 'stuck' child finally let go, calm down and comply. For example:

> 'You wanted to paint on the wall.' (Empathic reflection.)
> 'One thing we can't do is paint on the wall.' (Setting the limit using neutral language to protect self-esteem.)
> 'Let's find some paper — would you like white paper or yellow paper?'

Highlighting the choices your child is making can also help them understand the consequences of their choices. It can make the link between decisions and the outcomes of those decisions very clear. This means that, over time, children will be less likely to make excuses, and more likely to own their choices.

> *Child:* 'But I want to paint on the wall!!'
> *Dad:* 'If you choose to paint on the wall, you are choosing to have no paints today.'
> *Child:* 'I don't want paper! You can't make me!'
> *Dad:* 'You wish you could paint on the wall, but that's something we can't do.'

(Child paints on the wall.)

Dad: 'Looks like you've chosen to have no paints today.' (Parent removes paints.)

Child: 'Nooo! I'm sorry Daddy, I won't do it again! Don't take the paints...'

Dad: 'You wish you'd made a different choice.' (Highlighting the consequence of the choice.)

Child: 'Pleeeaase Daddy!'

Dad: 'The paints will be back tomorrow. Would you like to draw with the pencils or play with Lego?' (Remaining consistent with the consequences, offering choices to help calm.)

CHAPTER 9

Creating therapeutic play sessions:
'Special play time'

Angela North

Play therapy is a mindfulness-based psychotherapy for children, effective because it uses the child's language — the language of play. Can you imagine trying to sit a three year old in a chair and expecting them to reflect on their emotions, or answer questions, like you might with an older person? Even older children can be more comfortable *showing* their inner world through play, rather than using words. Children reveal a great deal about their internal struggles, beliefs and wishes through play, and mindful responses can harness these revelations to help the child heal, grow and connect.

In the 1960s, two American psychologists created a new

therapy that caused more than one raised eyebrow. Together, Dr Louise Guerney and Dr Bernard Guerney developed Filial Therapy (also known as 'Child Parent Relationship Therapy'), providing play therapy training to parents and giving them the ability to practise these techniques with their own children. In a weekly, 30-minute play session held at home, parents apply these skills to strengthen resilience, build close relationships, improve behaviours and help their child heal from trauma. Some of those strategies, such as empathic reflections, are contained in this book.

Critics challenged the idea that parents could make a difference in this way.[1] They were wrong. Research across cultures, different family structures and behavioural problems proved that Filial Therapy makes a significant difference that lasts.[2]

Some research demonstrates that in comparison to trained play therapists, parents who utilize Filial Therapy can be even more effective, because the advantages spread to the entire family.[3] You might wonder how this is possible but consider: a parent and their child need no time to 'get to know each other'. The parent is present, responding in therapeutic ways, day after day and in many different contexts. In comparison, a therapist might see the child once a week for an hour, and only in the context of a clinic. With parents, the child has an immersive experience — and with the most important person in their life. Best of all, children can gain rapid benefits, leaving parents feeling empowered to face parenting challenges with confidence. They can use these skills time and time again, at each point of the child's life. They will serve both parent and child throughout the teen years and beyond.

While training in Filial Therapy must be provided by a suitably qualified mental health professional, parents can harness many of the mindful, play-based strategies in this book to provide a therapeutic space for their child. Curious to know how your child might respond? Read on …

There are three rubber ducks lying on the floor among a circle of toys placed there for 'special play time'. Charlie lifts the smallest one into the air and flies it around the room. Suddenly, his chubby three-year-old fingers spread wide, and the duck drops to the floor. 'Oh no!' cries Charlie. 'The baby duck can't breathe!' An ambulance arrives, pushed hastily across the floorboards, siren wailing through high-pitched vocal cords. 'EEE-AWWW EEE-AWWW.' There is doll furniture in this circle, including a bed, but interestingly Charlie selects the oven, which has a plastic, see-through window. The 'baby duck' is placed inside, and Charlie turns to me. In a voice that sounds older, certainly more sombre, Charlie explains the sad tale: the duck is sick, that 'giant hands' will look after it for a while, and that eventually it can go home. Charlie adds that the duck has lost its family now: its mother doesn't know where it is, and so it goes home with a different mother.

Charlie will repeat a version of this story every week, for many, many months. It looks strangely like a re-telling of Charlie's birth, complete with isolation in a glass humidic-rib and difficulty in breathing. Charlie has never been told that story, but we know that much of trauma is stored in the mind and body, even before a child can speak. Charlie introduces subtle changes to the story, so that eventually the tables are turned. Where once the baby duck was ill, alone and scared, he becomes strong, recruiting family and friends and his own voice to counter obstacles. This is what play therapists' term 'reaching mastery' — where the play themes reflect the child's inner recovery, so that traumatic events and emotional struggles are integrated. Charlie's parents notice a change in behaviours at other times in the week that support this idea of recovery. One thing is for certain — the story has great meaning to Charlie, and *something* is being worked through.

Special play time

Conducting regular play sessions at home with your child can maximize your mindfulness practice and provide plenty of benefits to you and your child. Often referred to as 'special play time', these sessions are helpful for children between the ages of three and twelve. At twelve years of age (give or take), children will begin to use imaginary play less, and seek other forms of play more typical of the teenage years. If your child is already disinterested in imaginary play with toys, then you will find alternative ways to connect in the chapter on teenagers later in this book. If you are inspired to create a space for therapeutic play at home, read the checklist below to ensure that you have the time, energy and resources.

Is it doable for me, at this time? A checklist

Excited about special play time? Check here first, to ensure this is the right time for you and your child.

A regular and reliable time

Play sessions are most beneficial when they are offered at the same time every week. Some parents prefer a daily, five-minute play session, whereas others find that 30 minutes once a week suits them best. Regardless of what you choose, it is the reliability of this time that makes the difference. Children love 'special play time' and will look forward to it with an intensity that might surprise you. Importantly, they will bring their worries, fears and frustrations to these sessions. If the session is cancelled unexpectedly, it can increase their distress.

Uninterrupted parent–child time

Special play time creates a bubble of time, where all other things are put aside, and the relationship between you and your child is prioritized. Phones are turned off and siblings are cared for by others (or old enough to resist interrupting). Many children experience their parents as busy and distracted. Indeed, some behavioural problems arise when children solve their need for attention by whining, crying, becoming aggressive or other challenging behaviours. Special play time can help children meet that need in a healthier way. You can emphasize this feature of special play time by enlisting your child to help you with the following:

- Let your child decide on a name. It could be 'special play time' or 'special Mum/Dad time' or any other name they decide.
- Create a 'do not disturb' sign for the front door (or the room where the play will occur). Each play session, place it on the door, turn off your phone and make it clear that this is special, uninterrupted time with your child.

Special play time toys

Special play time requires a small selection of toys specifically chosen for their ability to invite expression and creativity. If possible, these toys will be kept separate, accessible only during special play time. A comprehensive list and explanatory notes for their inclusion can be found in the resources section of this book. It is important to note that, ideally, items should not be new, as worry about scratching/damaging new toys can prevent parents and children from feeling truly free to play in the way that they wish to. Inexpensive, second-hand toys from charity/thrift/opportunity shops are ideal. Children will gravitate to the toys that best express their needs, wishes, wants and feelings at that moment in time.

Tick, tick and tick — I'm ready

You've read the checklist and feel able and inspired to create a special play time with your child. Below you will find many guidelines for maximizing the benefits of this time, but the number one priority is to follow your child's lead … and have fun.

Allocating time and space

Decide what day(s) and time you can comfortably commit to uninterrupted special play time. How long will it be? Where is the best space? If there are other people in the home, is there a space that will be private, and where your child can be free to engage in boisterous play without risk of damaging furniture or hurting themselves? Some examples of special play time structures include:

- Thirty minutes of play, every Saturday morning, on the dining room floor (maximum space, no fragile items nearby).
- Five minutes of play, every day after school, immediately after you've shared a snack, on the back veranda.
- Ten minutes of play on Saturday and Wednesday mornings, in the family room (lamp removed for safety).

Find, make or purchase a selection of toys

See a full list of options in the resources section of this book.

Introduce your child to the idea of special play time

Here is an example of how you could introduce your child to the concept of special play time.

'Niko, I have been learning about something called "special play time" and I think you would like it. We would spend ten minutes after dinner every day, playing with a box of toys that are only for this time. How does that sound?'

Set up the toys

Set the toys up before special play time begins, preferably without your child present. The toys can be placed in a circle, and you might like to add a rug or towel if messy play is included (such as paint, water or playdough). However you choose to arrange the toys (e.g. doll and doll clothes together, craft paper, paints, pencils and playdough together), try to create the same arrangement every time. This consistency can be helpful for children, enabling them to quickly find the items they need once they are accustomed to the layout.

Introduction

Here's a scenario of how you could introduce special play time to your child.

> *Parent:* 'Here we are in special play time, Niko. You can choose to play in whatever ways you would like to.'
> (Niko immediately runs to the cars he sees grouped together.) 'This is great! I love this one!'
> *Parent:* 'You're pretty excited — sounds like that one is your favourite.'

Empathic reflections and setting limits

Reflect the emotions, wishes and wants that your child expresses during their play. If you need to set a limit, remember to use neutral language that protects self-esteem (see Chapter 8). During special play time, we want to minimize the amount of limit-setting that we need to do. We achieve this by including toys that can withstand physical play (or are easily replaced), removing fragile items from the space while playing, and prioritizing only those limits that relate to our child's safety, our safety, and the deliberate destruction of toys. If your child has a strong need/wish to be destructive, provide options for these in the toy kit, such as egg cartons that can be stomped on, sticks that can be snapped or bubble-wrap that can be popped.

> *Niko:* 'Oh wow — there's water! Can I put the cars in the water?'
>
> *Parent:* 'You'd like to put the cars in there. That's something you can do! And if there's something you can't do, I'll let you know.'
> (Niko gathers all the plastic cars and puts them in the container of water.)
>
> *Niko:* 'Can I put the playdough in there too?'
>
> *Parent:* 'You'd like the playdough to go in there. One thing we can't do is put playdough in the water. But you wish you could.'
>
> *Niko:* 'But I want to!'
>
> *Parent:* 'You're sad about that — you wish you could put playdough in there.'
>
> *Niko:* 'Well … can you make a house for the cars? I'm gonna make a playdough car.'

121

Allow your child to stay in the lead and track their play with your words

Follow your child's lead in play. If they wish you to simply observe, then you can still emphasize your focus by sitting close by and making occasional comments about what you're seeing. Even when a child plays silently, your verbal 'tracking' of their play lets them know that they have your full attention. It also allows you to reflect any feelings, wishes or wants that are evident in the play. Children's play will reveal the issues they are wrestling with. In play, they can give themselves what they cannot have in reality — this can be very healing, and helps children cope with reality in more constructive ways.

(Niko sits quietly with the tray of dry rice. He has chosen some people figurines and is laying them on top of the rice.)

Parent: 'You're deciding which people to put there.'

(Niko pushes a baby figurine into the rice until it disappears.)

Parent: 'You made that one disappear.'

(Niko smiles.) 'That's Ari.' (Ari is Niko's baby brother.)

Parent: 'You made Ari disappear, and that makes you smile.'

(One by one, Niko sinks the other figurines, naming each as he goes.)

Niko: 'Daddy, Cousin Joe, Breanna. Now it's just you and me, Mummy!'

Parent: 'You made everyone disappear and now it's just us.'

Niko: 'Yeah! We could have special play time all the time.'

Parent: 'You would really like that — having me all to yourself, all the time.'

Role playing

Of course, many times, children will want you to play with them. Consider them the 'director' of their own show, with you following their instructions.

Ending special play time

Children will benefit from a five-minute (and possibly a one-minute) warning before the end of special play time, as this transition can be challenging for them. You may decide to help the transition by providing a special snack ritual afterwards, such as 'after every special play time, we will have a hot chocolate'. However, keep in mind that special play time is designed to help children learn the difficult task of managing big feelings (emotion regulation), and the end of the play session is an opportunity to support that growth. If a child refuses to finish, use your empathic reflections to acknowledge their wish. Be patient, allow a few minutes to pass as they grapple with self-control. If necessary, tidy up the toys and put them away, while continuing to empathically reflect their struggle. At this stage, you might also like to provide a choice to help your child become 'unstuck'. For example:

Parent: 'Niko, I know you wish you could keep playing, but special play time has finished for today. You can choose to come and have a hot chocolate or go outside to play. Which do you choose?'

Niko: 'I want special play time!'

Parent: 'Special play time is not one of the choices. You can choose hot chocolate, or outside play. Which do you choose?'

Packing up

If your child wants to help pack up, then you can encourage and thank them for their help (thanking children is a wonderful way of bringing mindful attention to any positive, pro-social acts). However, children are generally not required to assist in cleaning up after therapeutic play sessions. The reason for this is that these play sessions are designed to create a permissive space where the full range of feelings, wishes and wants can be expressed. For example, a child who is angry at the separation of their parents may want to tear pieces of paper into small pieces and throw it around the room. This act can be cathartic — a release of emotions that would otherwise stay bottled up. If the child knows that they are responsible for cleaning up, however, over time they will be less likely to engage in messy play.

Encouragement versus praise

When we praise a child for a successful outcome, they might feel (temporarily) nice — pleased that we like what we see. However, over time our praise is teaching them to focus on what pleases others. They will quickly lose motivation if they do not receive regular praise to keep them going.

Occasional praise for a job well done is not a problem. But

success in life requires persistence — usually without any fan club cheering us on. The alternative is to focus on *effort*. When we draw our child's attention to the effort they have put in, we are encouraging them to look inwards and feel pride. Unlike the temporary warmth that stems from other people's praise, the pride that comes from persistence is in the *child's* control. This means they can access a genuine sense of pride whenever they want or need to. Their self-esteem is in their hands. Here are some examples:

> **You're feeling so proud of your picture!**
> **You're figuring that out.**
> **You're determined to work that out.**
> **You're thinking of lots of ways to make that work.**
> **You worked it out!**
> **I can see you've spent a lot of time on that.**

Themes of play

As children spend time acting out their experiences, feelings, beliefs and wishes in the safe environment of special play time, parents will notice patterns emerging. These patterns, or themes, can give us a rich insight into the inner life of our child. They provide clues to our child's struggles, and as those themes shift and change, we are witnessing our child's path to resolution.

A theme is evident when a child repeatedly chooses a certain toy or particular activity over several play sessions. Examples of common themes are good versus evil, control and power versus powerlessness, family relationships, winning and losing, grief, hopes, success and failure.

Noticing the themes that arise, and what these might mean for our child, gives us a unique opportunity to understand them. While we don't share our interpretations with our child, such insights can guide us in our parenting, and help us feel compassion and patience where once we might have felt only confusion and frustration. As themes evolve, we can directly observe the positive effect of our therapeutic work. In the space we have created, our child is healing and building resilience.

> Noah, a three-year-old boy, is struggling to manage the arrival of a sibling, expressing this with both clingy and aggressive behaviours at home. In special play time, he takes the smallest dinosaur toy, removes it from the other dinosaurs and repeatedly and aggressively piles blocks on top of it. After several sessions of this, Noah places the dinosaur back with its family, but does not allow it to eat the family meal. Still later, he gives the dinosaur 'a tiny bit of pasta'. It is a small concession for the dinosaur, and a giant leap for Noah, towards acceptance of his sibling.

> Alice is six years old and has shown symptoms of anxiety since her parents separated twelve months earlier. In special play time, she delights in ordering her father to obey her every wish. At times, she dresses as a wizard and uses her wand to grant her own wishes. These

include being 'the boss of her parents'. Initially, her play is intense and highly controlling. She is very tired after each session. Eventually, she begins to engage in other, more creative play themes, including drawing a picture for her father. She even allows her father to have a turn of the wand, and her play is less intense, more playful and humorous. After an initial peak, her anxiety symptoms have also diminished over this period of time.

Millie is eight years old. It is her first special play time, and she immediately empties the entire contents of the playdough tub onto the table. She spends several minutes rolling the dough into a large ball.

> *Parent:* 'You're making sure that's just the way you want it.'
> *Millie:* 'I'm making a big bowling ball! We're going to have a competition. Can you set up the bowling things?'
> *Parent:* 'You want me to line these up. Okay, they're ready.'
> (Millie pinches a tiny amount of play-dough and rolls it into a ball the size of a matchhead. She hands it to her mother.)
> *Millie:* 'Here's *your* ball mummy! Let's see who wins.'

Parent: 'Looks like you really want to win this competition. You've made a big ball for you, and a tiny ball for me.'

Millie giggles, delighting in the freedom to be 'the boss' in special play time. In here, her competitive spirit can be unfettered by issues of fairness or manners. Millie proceeds to win several competitions, laughing at her mother's attempts to roll a tiny ball of playdough. Each time it lands on the floor with no effect, there is a great deal of laughter from both mother and daughter. After a while, it seems Millie's need to win is satisfied. In a calmer state than when she first began special play time, she hands the large playdough ball to her mother.

Millie: 'You can have the big ball now, Mummy.'
Parent: 'You've decided to let me win, too.'
Millie: 'Yeah, you can win too. Then can we play dolls?'

Interested in Filial Therapy training?

Many of the strategies outlined in this book are key elements of Filial Therapy. If you are interested in exploring this approach further, please see the note at the end of this book under 'resources', to help you find appropriate training.

CHAPTER 10

Teenagers:
Saying goodbye to childhood

Angela North

'Forget it.'
'I'm leaving.'
'You're not my dad.'
'I wish you were dead.'
'I didn't ask to be born.'
'You don't understand.'
'Don't tell me how to live my life!'

Raising teenagers is not for the faint-hearted. It is for those with big hearts, full of understanding, patience, humility and humour. Not the bitter humour of simmering frustration, but the humour that comes from remembering what we did when *we* were teenagers.

Saying goodbye to childhood

Parenting a teenager is a process of letting go. Depending on your own life circumstances and teenage experiences, this can be painful. Some parents rejoice in their child's growing strengths and independence. Other parents experience waves of fear at the risks that come with independence. Still others feel grief, perhaps recalling the years when their bedtime stories, wisdom and company were so highly valued. Often, it is a combination of all these things, and we can whiplash from one to the other in the space of an hour. It helps to mindfully acknowledge our joy, fear, grief and other emotions, as we leave sippy cups, favourite blankies, gap-toothed smiles and giggles behind.

When we have a child, most of us develop a picture of how the teenage years will look, whether we are consciously aware of it or not. Here are some examples:

'I'm going to be the "hippy earth mother", with lots of laughter and music in the house, and lots of baking. My teenager's friends will want to hang out here — our house will be full of teens and food. One thing I'm sure of — kids love food!'

'When my boys are teenagers, I'll keep them safe by keeping them busy — lots of sport, which was a big thing when I was growing up. It gives you a great community to be part of, and it teaches you about life in a fun way — the importance of teamwork, of showing up.'

'I'm going to make sure my teenagers don't make the same mistakes I did. I want them to study hard, go to university.'

When reality differs from this picture, we can get stuck. Invariably, we overestimate our control during this period and underestimate life's habit of being utterly different to how we imagined it. We are trying to control the uncontrollable. This can cause a great deal of tension — between what *is* and what we *imagined* — and sometimes our teenagers suffer the sting of our misdirected frustration.

There is an old Yiddish proverb: 'We plan, God laughs.' Things have a way of turning out a little differently to what we expected — the 'earth mother' is too busy to bake, the son has no interest in sport, and a teenager decides that university is not for them.

Our ability to manage our teenager's needs with grace will depend on how willing we are to let go of the fantasy we have created. Mindfulness can release us from this unhappy prison of our own making. Only then will we discover the gifts of the person in front of us. In being too busy to bake, the earth mother has instead found passion in her career and is still a beautiful role model for her children, just in a different way. The son who has no interest in sport is also kind, funny and shares his grandmother's natural gift with words. The teenager who is uninspired by university decides to travel and, in doing so, meets a need for adventure and cultural curiosity.

Mindfulness releases us from a rigid attachment to old imaginings, so we don't miss the delights of the reality in front of us.

Managing expectations

'Grow up! You're behaving like a child!' Have you ever heard either of your parents say that to you or caught yourself saying it to one of your own children? Take the age of your child and subtract ten years. That age range — from three to thirteen years, for example — is your guide to the behaviours you might expect. Your thirteen-year-old will occasionally seem more like a three-year-old — big tantrums, big tears, not much logic. Your eighteen-year-old has a greater capacity for reason but will still occasionally behave like an eight year old when under stress.

Why do behaviours swing so widely? The developmental challenges teenagers face are huge. Ever notice that in times of stress, *you* get forgetful, miss appointments you would normally remember, struggle to find simple words to express yourself, snap at people when you'd normally be patient, and throw childlike tantrums (at least in your head)? That's regression. Occasionally our teens will also regress — reverting to an earlier time of development — a 'two steps forward, one step back' dance.

Regression is something we all do at times and, like everyone when they are overwhelmed, the solution is compassion and time. Your teenager will need both.

This is awkward

Developmentally, the teenage years are a complex and messy time for your child. Teens are forming an identity and often feel insecure, unsure of their place in their friendship groups, and in society generally. They live with an almost constant sense of impermanence and uncertainty. Their bodies are suddenly and rapidly changing, signalling new challenges: hormones, body image, romantic relationships and sexual identity, to name a few.

This is a sensitive period of growth, with identity and social standing at stake. Many teenagers are self-conscious and easily embarrassed. As a result, they may be hyper-aware of perceived rejection and, at the same time, determined to appear as if they don't care. They do. Find as many strengths and positives as you can, big or small, and name them as frequently as you can. Your appreciation for a song they like, an outfit they put together, a new friend they've made, or a joke that made you laugh out loud can be a much-needed salve in this time.

Out of our depth

One thing is for certain: almost every teenager will present a problem that their parent has never experienced — perhaps never even imagined. Life in the last 25 years has changed dramatically, and so the pattern continues. In her song, 'We can do hard things', Tish Melton, daughter of author and activist Glennon Doyle, says, 'I've stopped asking directions to places they've never been.' Parents will sometimes rush to advise, reassure or guide. But we are offering directions with no lived experience of the problem.

When our children reveal significant things to us, we can feel an overwhelming rush of emotions. We might recognize immediately that *this is a big moment*. Our next thought might be DON'T STUFF THIS UP. If we are alarmed or shocked, we might go immediately to the 'roadblocks' discussed earlier — all those responses that block the flow of conversation, leading our child to anger or retreat. Even if our values and beliefs aren't being challenged, most parents feel a need to end their child's suffering through reassurance, offering a quick, knee-jerk 'it's fine/you're fine/this will pass' reaction. Sadly, this only serves as an emotional bandaid smothering our child's feelings and concerns with platitudes. Somehow, we must maintain connection while respecting the need for space that is a hallmark of the teenage years.

A little distance, please

During this period, teenagers crave independence from parental values and rules. How can they clearly see who they are — and who they wish to become — if they are still deferring to your ideas, your values and your ways of thinking? A little distance allows them to experiment with alternative ideas, interests and identities. They may make many changes to their style, musical tastes, study and career plans, cultural identity and friendships, among other things.

Psychologists call this important part of development *differentiation*. If you are not prepared for it, this period can be full of conflict. You might find yourself treating every point of difference as a personal rejection. Your sadness, frustration or fear might be expressed in unhelpful ways, such as sarcasm, or 'playful' teasing about body changes, music interests and so forth. To the self-conscious teen, this will only increase feelings of embarrassment and anger, leading to conflict or withdrawal.

Strategies for maintaining connection

Empathic reflections provide a safe space for the self-conscious teenager, keeping and strengthening the connection that is still there. It may not seem like it, but your empathy is needed more than ever. Empathic reflections validate the marathon of emotions, relationships, and identity shifts experienced by teenagers. Development of identity requires your teen to emotionally move away for a while. Empathic reflections will help them find their way home.

When your teenager is upset or angry

Especially when your teen's emotional temperature is rising, your willingness to follow their lead with compassion and curiosity increases the chance that you will get the full picture. This simply means you express empathy and go where their responses take you, rather than directing the conversation yourself. 'Roadblocks' like problem solving and judgement will stop a conversation in its tracks. Empathic reflections are the alternative that provide safety for teenagers who still need and want your acceptance, but also need space to work out their own solutions. If you are concerned about their safety and want open communication to discuss it, you must first create emotional safety.

PARENT 'ROADBLOCK' COMMENTS	EMPATHIC REFLECTIONS AND FOLLOWING THEIR LEAD
Well, what did you expect?!	**That sounds tough.**
I can't believe you did that. How many times have I told you ...?	**I'm sorry to hear that. Sounds like you've got some regrets.**
You should break up with him: I never liked him anyway.	**I see you've got mixed feelings about him. Be kind to yourself – it might take some time to work out what you want.**
What the hell did they say? I would never let someone speak to me like that!	**So, what did you think about that comment?**
Who cares what they think? You're better than that.	**I get it – sometimes we lose sight of our own worth. We all want to be liked at times.**
Don't listen to them, they're idiots.	**You want to be part of the group, but it sounds like it's costing you a lot.**
Be a leader, not a follower. Just tell her what you think.	**It's hard to be assertive sometimes, I know.**
Don't tell me you're not angry mister! I've known you your whole life.	**Oh okay, I got that wrong.**

You may recall from your own teenage years how self-conscious and sensitive this period can be. Advice that would have been tolerated (or even enthusiastically received!) by a younger child is easily interpreted as criticism by a teenager. Refraining from teasing or offering unwanted advice is an act of compassion parents can easily miss. And, despite the parenting beliefs of previous generations, you can't 'tease' a person out of sensitivity. Using emotional and psychological strategies that ignore or make fun of a teenager's autonomy and preferences is directly connected to the development of depression, not resilience.[1] In other words, they won't 'toughen up'; they will fight you or retreat, and it could cost them their mental health.

With teenagers, conversations won't come as frequently nor as enthusiastically as they once did. You can create opportunities, however, by harnessing your teen's interests and their natural inclination to talk more when they feel less scrutinized.

'Just you and me' time

If possible, have a regular outing that you can do with your teenager that is purely for fun. It might be a trip to their favourite cafe, or wandering around the shops, or a hike if they're nature buffs. Make a commitment to yourself that conversations during these outings will be led by your child. 'Let them lead' is discussed in the previous chapter on special play times and the philosophy applies here too.

For this to work, you will do a lot of listening, empathic reflections, expressing curiosity about their thoughts or ideas and *leaving your own thoughts and ideas aside unless directly asked*. If you can make this a regular and reliable time together, it can be especially therapeutic. Sometimes it will be light-hearted, chatty and full of humour; other times may result in deeper and more personal discussions.

'Side-by-side' time

As any parent who has been 'taxi' for their child can attest, the most revealing conversations happen when you and your teenager are not face to face, but actually side by side. Teenagers talk more openly and easily at these times as they can feel less self-conscious when not observed. Take advantage of these opportunities when they occur, such as in the car, while walking, cooking, sharing chores or watching a game together. If you need to raise a concern your teen is reluctant to discuss, you might acknowledge their reluctance and give them time to prepare. For example:

> **'I understand this is hard to talk about. I am concerned and want to make sure you're okay. If you don't want to talk about it now, that's fine, but I'd like you to think of a time when we can talk.'**

Everyday conversations with your teenager can support connection, so that there are many moments full of laughter, anecdotes and, occasionally, deeper discussions about important issues. It is easy to believe that teens are averse to such connection. While it is true that this period of development requires more space and independence, parents often unwittingly sabotage connection with 'roadblocks' such as pointed questions, insensitive teasing, unwanted problem solving and judgement. See below for two examples of such a conversation, the first with 'roadblocks' and the second with empathic reflections.

EXAMPLE 1: COMMUNICATION ROAD-BLOCKS WITH NO EMPATHIC REFLECTIONS

Teen: 'Can I have a toasted sandwich and a frappe?'

Parent: 'Sure — I didn't know you liked coffee.'

Teen: 'Yeah, Kaylee got me onto them. She's obsessed.'

Parent: 'Ooh, Kaylee huh? Anything you wanna tell me about Kaylee …'

Teen: (scowls) 'She's just a friend, Dad.'

Parent: 'Sure, that's what they *all* say.' (laughs)

Teen: 'Forget it.'

Parent: 'Don't be like that! I'm just joking.' (silence)

Parent: 'So, how's school?'

Teen: 'Okay.'

Parent: 'Yeah? How's the gang going? Haven't seen much of them.'

Teen: 'They're okay. Busy with work and stuff.'

Parent: 'Oh, okay.'

EXAMPLE 2: COMMUNICATION WITH EMPATHIC REFLECTIONS AND NO ROAD-BLOCKS

Teen: 'Can I have a toasted sandwich and a frappe?'

Parent: 'Sure — I didn't know you liked coffee.'

Teen: 'Yeah, Kaylee got me onto them. She's obsessed.'

Parent: 'Smart girl — coffee is my superpower! She's the new girl at school?'

Teen: 'Yep.'

Parent: 'Cool. How's she settling in? It can't be easy, starting new in the middle of Year 10.'

Teen: 'She's cool — and she knew Tim from primary school, so …'

Parent: 'That makes it easier, for sure. Tim hasn't come around for a while, or the rest of the mob.'

Teen: (smirks) 'You wanna hang out with the cool kids, Dad?'

Parent: (laughs) 'You're worried I'll stick around and be all awkward. Nah, if you want to have your mates over, I promise I'll leave you with the music and the pizzas. Mum and I will hog the TV in the front room. Up to you.'

Teen: 'Yeah, might be good. I'll ask around. Dunno about Tim though. He's been weird lately.'

Parent: 'Sorry to hear that. What's going on?'

Teen: 'He's just being an idiot. Doing stupid things, not turning up to school. He doesn't hang with us as much.'

Parent: 'When I think "stupid things", I think maybe drugs, stealing, hanging with a bad crowd, that kind of thing …'

Teen: 'Yeah, he's been smoking weed a bit. Drinks a lot. Even turned up at school stoned.'

Parent: 'Sounds like he's struggling, that's for sure. Anyone helping him out?'

Teen: 'I don't think so. He'd never talk to his parents.'

Parent: 'How are you feeling about it?'

Teen: 'I dunno. A bit worried. Kinda miss the old Tim, too.'

Parent: 'Yeah, you guys have been good friends for ages. What's your biggest concern?'

Teen: 'Maybe he's depressed. He said as much. You know, like "Life is bullshit, I don't wanna do this anymore" — lots of stuff like that.'

Parent: 'It does sound like he could do with some help. I don't think you should carry this on your own. Sometimes you've got to hand stuff over to adults — especially if it's about someone's safety. How do you feel about that?'

Teen: 'He'll hate me if he knew I'd said something!'

Parent: 'I'm sure we can let people in Tim's life know that he needs help, without you being mentioned. How about I investigate what the options are, and run them by you, before I contact anyone?'

Teen: '... sure, okay.'

Finding time to spend with your teenager one on one, avoiding roadblocks to open communication, prioritizing empathic reflections and following their lead in conversations: these are the ways in which we keep the door to open communication wide open. When we do, we create opportunities to support our teenagers through tough times, even if that support is simply listening and being present while they struggle. Best of all, we are rewarded with a closer relationship than the 'accepted wisdom' of the teenage years would suggest possible.

Inspiring future adults

'As much as we watch to see what our children do with their lives, they are watching us to see what we do with ours. I can't tell my children to reach for the sun. All I can do is reach for it, myself.'

Joyce Maynard, author

Mindful parenting directs our attention to the here and now, so that our teenagers will feel our presence and support is truly authentic. However, given the adventures that lie ahead for them, teenagers also need to see that the adulthood on their horizon is worth working towards.

Tune in to the average parent's conversations and you might notice a negative focus on bills, job stress, annoying family members, the cost of living, and how very, very tired/busy/fed-up parents are.

There is a current culture of pride in being busy, as if our value is in what we *do* — how much we can cram into a day. We wipe our brow, rush around doing errands, picking up kids, getting meals ready and chores done. All the while, we complain of exhaustion. Hardly a great advertising campaign! But the solution will surprise and (likely) delight you. It is self-care.

Mindfulness invites us to make a deliberate choice, to be more present for our *own* lives, and the lives of our children. The next time you find yourself apologizing for taking a moment to yourself, stop and reframe the conversation: 'I love having a bath when I need a rest. I'm going to do the whole "luxury spa" thing — candles, music, my book.'

Your teenager notices when you are looking after yourself, enjoying your life and having a good laugh. Commenting on the things you love about your life, the things you are grateful for, as well as your strengths and passions, helps create awareness and optimism in your teen. *Showing* them, through self-care, exercise, hobbies, time with friends, or dancing in the kitchen to your favourite music, is even more powerful. You are *living* the message: that adulthood is worth it.

A man in his thirties participated in a 'positive psychology' research study. He scored particularly high on 'life satisfaction' and was later interviewed about his childhood. Raised by a single mum, he always felt loved. But what was most notable was that his mother did not spend a huge amount of time focusing on his activities and interests. He described her as living a full and joyful life — someone who loved her work, family, friends and hobbies. While they struggled financially at times, he said he never felt deprived. In fact, he could see, through his mother's eyes, that adulthood might be interesting and worthwhile. She inspired his own attitude to life.

From authority figure to trusted advisor

Mindfulness offers many ways to approach the transition from *authority figure* to *trusted advisor*. You might focus on developing your ability to stay calm so that you can be the thermostat that switches off when your teen is getting emotionally heated. Perhaps you will seek more regular opportunities for connection: following your teen's lead, utilizing empathic reflections and changing the quality of these conversations. The notion of being a role model for adulthood may have already inspired ideas for prioritising greater joy and self-care in your own life.

And because mindfulness is about accepting reality, you will walk this path knowing that, at times, you will still find yourself rattled, like every parent of a teenager before you. The internet, gender identity, sexual relationships, drugs and alcohol are just a few of the subjects that leave parents feeling unprepared and overwhelmed. 'Just tell me what to say' is possibly the most common refrain of parents seeking guidance about their teens. While *what to say* will depend to some degree on your values, beliefs and culture, one thing is for certain — your capacity to stay calm, listen and take time to understand will *always* benefit. In the following chapter, we take a deeper dive into some of these more complex issues, such as how we can be a much-needed safety net while ensuring that our teens are building their own ability to assess risk.

CHAPTER 11

Teenagers and independence (with a safety net)

Angela North

Let's explore some of the more challenging moments in detail, such as those times when your teen might need, or even welcome, a non-judgemental advisor.

The internet

Teenagers are facing challenges and opportunities that previous generations did not through access to the internet, and social media in particular. Critics of social media highlight the risks: bullying; anxiety from the fear of missing out; the curated 'perfection' that leaves teens feeling body image and life dissatisfaction; predatory behaviour; and the prevalence of convincing but inaccurate information.

There are, however, some benefits to social media, including access to like-minded communities, opportunities to explore hobbies and interests, and a growing language for social commentary on important issues. Indeed, teens are more aware than previous generations about personal and global issues that affect their future. Politics, gender and racial inequality, global warming and mental health are just some examples of issues where teens have made their feelings and opinions known.

Parental involvement can balance the scales between risk and inspiration. Limiting access to the internet is increasingly difficult as your child gets older, particularly with the advent of smart phones and the broad use of computers for school-related participation. However, it presents a new opportunity for you — to become the student.

An increasing number of teenagers can speak to important matters in ways we could not. Setting aside a stance of 'authority' might feel uncomfortable, especially when you have been the source of knowledge and advice for many years. However, a willingness to listen to your teen's growing knowledge about their interests and worldview is a wonderful way to build closeness and understanding — and you might be delighted to learn a new perspective on the world. Ask them about their interest in music, fashion, identity and friendships (with curiosity and an open mind). Listen to their ideas about culture, feminism, social media trends and so forth.

It's helpful to monitor your tone in these conversations: your teen will be acutely attuned to the difference between genuine interest and being patronized or criticized. If you are struggling to understand and feeling out of your depth, mindfully recognize in yourself how this might be expressed as anger or fear. Be compassionate to yourself — you might even invite your child to help. For example, 'This stuff is completely new to me. It frightens me a little. Can you help me understand it a bit better?'

Identity and gender

Mindfulness provides a path to greater inclusion for those who are marginalized due to their colour, culture, religion, disability, gender identity or sexuality. In a state of acceptance, we do not seek to change or judge. Instead, we are present and compassionate for the struggles of our child.

As a result of their treatment in society, marginalized children and teens suffer poorer mental health in comparison to others. Our ability to respond in inclusive and affirming ways can make a profound difference. Below is an example of a conversation between a mother and her child who identifies as non-binary (i.e. neither male nor female), while they were walking home from the train station one day.

> *Mum:* 'Are you okay? You seem kind of quiet …'
> *Teen:* 'I dunno. I felt crappy all day at school.'
> *Mum:* 'All day — that must have been tough.'
> *Teen:* 'I just … I wish I wasn't wearing this outfit.'
> *Mum:* 'Something about the outfit is bothering you?'
> *Teen:* 'I hate this skirt. It felt wrong. Sometimes I feel like a girl and sometimes I feel like a boy

— or neither. And I feel like *I should know by now*. There's all this pressure in my head, like "decide! decide!". But I really don't know who I am.'

Mum: 'I'm so sorry. That's a big thing to be wrestling with.'

Teen: (sigh)

Mum: 'Would it be okay to share some thoughts, in case any of them make sense to you?'

Teen: 'Yeah, okay.'

Mum: 'It sounds like you're expecting to know who you are, at sixteen. You're really giving yourself a hard time about this.'

Teen: 'That doesn't sound like me!' (laughs).

Mum: 'So, I wonder, perhaps you could give yourself permission to *not* know — to let it be, set it aside and trust that what is true for you will keep getting clearer over time.'

Teen: 'Yeah, maybe …'

Mum: 'Because I'm not sure we can speed up the making of our identity! But we can be kind to ourselves while we're figuring it out.'

Teen: (silence)

Mum: 'In the meantime, each day you can dress according to how you feel. Boy, girl or neither.'

Teen: 'Yeah, that makes sense. Thanks, Mum. (hugs) Honestly, I can't wait to get home and get my androgynous gear on!'

Parents may feel very unsure how to respond to issues of gender, sex and sexuality — topics that many find difficult to discuss, even in more typical circumstances. Regardless of the topic, if your teenager is brave enough to raise it, prioritize listening and understanding in that moment. In the example above, the mother's mindful parenting included a gentle reminder for her teen to slow down (by coming back to the present moment instead of worrying about the future) and to be self-compassionate. Studies with sexual- and gender-diverse teenagers has found that self-compassion is particularly effective for building resilience against stigma.[1]

Your first response can be as simple as 'Thank you for telling me that. I suspect it took a lot of courage. Would you like to tell me more?' When we are not in a mindful state, we habitually rush in, ready to respond with a bunch of 'roadblocks' in the form of questions, criticisms or anecdotes designed to teach a moral lesson.

And if we truly have stumbled onto new territory, we can give ourselves time while honouring the importance of the conversation, by stating something along the lines of 'I think this is important, and I'm grateful you shared it with me. Would it be okay to talk about it again?' Or even more simply, 'What do you need right now?'

One final note about gender and sexuality. Many sexual- and gender-diverse teenagers experience family rejection. As a result of this, and the experiences of discrimination in the broader community, these teens are at greater risk of homelessness, family violence, mental health issues and substance abuse. Thankfully, many parents recognize that their acceptance is critical to their teenager's ability to thrive. If your child needs such reassurance, you might be inclined to say, 'Don't worry, I still love you,' or something similar. Your compassion is needed. However, it is worth nothing that this is the same language we use when our teen has made a mistake, broken a rule or somehow 'failed' us. It suggests 'I love you *despite* this new information'. If your teen is courageous enough to talk to you with such vulnerable honesty, consider the following responses instead:

> 'Thanks for trusting me enough to share that with me.'

> 'It makes me happy to know that you are working out who you are. More than anything, I want that for you. I love you.'

> 'I love you, I'm proud of you, and I'm here whenever you want to talk about stuff. '

> 'It takes courage to be who we truly are. I am so proud of you. More importantly, I hope you're proud of yourself.'

Reminding ourselves that we do not need to 'fix' our child's problem can considerably relieve our parenting anxiety. In this space we are free to be authentic, present, without pressure. It can feel like a revelation! We forget that we can simply stop what we are doing, put down our phone/pen/ laptop, and listen closely. Mindfully.

Sexual relationships

Understandably, parents shy away from detailed discussions about sexual intimacy, either avoiding it altogether or trying to get the basics covered in a one-off speed-chat. Yet most parents imagine a future for their teenager that includes a loving and respectful partnership, and that includes intimacy.

We want our teen to build a healthy picture of intimacy *before* they embark on a sexual relationship. Discussions can and should cover a range of issues, including the 'basics': (consent, pregnancy, birth control, sexually transmitted diseases) and, equally importantly, pleasure. If we omit the latter (and many do), any gaps in information will be filled by friends (equally inexperienced teenagers), as well as media and pornography. Conversations should be private, and regular. If there is resistance, emphasise that your role is to ensure their health and safety, even if it means having awkward conversations. Humour at your own clumsiness can help! The aim is to maximize health, safety and a positive attitude towards intimacy with a trusted partner, for when the time comes. If you're not sure where to start, there are several modern books on dating, consent and sexual intimacy written for teens. Read one first before providing it to your teen; chances are you will pick up some great tips and develop greater comfort in discussing these topics.

Consent

Some teenagers engage in sexual relationships before they are emotionally ready. They may feel pressured and lack the skills or confidence to say no. They may not want to say no, because years of societal training has taught them that their value is measured by how desirable or wanted they are.

By the time children become teenagers, they may be well trained to judge themselves by what *other* people think, for example, 'They want me, so I must be worth something'. They have learned to fit in, moulding themselves to the group, rather than finding friends where their authentic self is respected and celebrated. There are many systemic and societal reasons for this, yet teenagers receive a great deal of negative press for their 'choices'. We ask them to face society's tidal wave of mixed messages with the confidence and knowledge many of us lack ourselves!

Below are some ideas to consider as your child or teen develops ideas about sexual relationships and, eventually, decisions about intimacy. You might like to discuss these with your teen and see what their thoughts are.

- From the beginning, teach your child that they can say no to adults. Respect their rights to their own bodies. 'It's okay if you don't want to kiss Grandma — you can say a friendly hello instead.'
- Refrain from comments that inadvertently sexualize children. Sexualized comments begin early: toddlers are told they're going to 'break hearts'; parents are told to 'start digging the moat' to protect their child; three year olds are teased about whether they have a girlfriend or boyfriend yet; high-heels and make-up are gifted to kindergarteners.
- If children want privacy when getting dressed, fully support this, regardless of age. Resist the urge to tease ('Ooh my little girl is growing up!' or 'Don't

worry — it's nothing I haven't seen before'). This may be their first experience of setting boundaries — welcome and celebrate it, so that setting boundaries about their body becomes a natural habit.

- Once your child has requested privacy, or they have reached late childhood/early teens, always ask before entering their private space such as a bedroom or bathroom (e.g. knock and wait for a response). Ask them to do the same for you.
- Build their awareness of their intrinsic worth by using empathic reflections that focus on strengths and interests, rather than appearance or innate intelligence, both of which are mostly out of your child's control.

My body, my rules

Consent should be explicitly discussed with all children and teenagers. It begins with an awareness for the child that their body is theirs alone, with the right to privacy when toileting, dressing and bathing. Your use of empathic reflections will benefit them also because it teaches them to tune inwards and ask, *What do I want*? When it comes to their own bodies, this is the most important question of all.

Enthusiastic consent

Ensure that your teenager understands the difference between a reluctant 'yes' and true consent. A quiet nod while looking shyly at the ground is not true consent. Engaging in intimacy with someone when affected by alcohol or drugs is not true consent. Some teenagers will enter their first sexual encounter because they simply don't have the skills or confidence to say, 'No, I'm not ready.' So, consent must be *enthusiastic*. Help your teen recognize enthusiastic consent in themselves and others. Teach them mindful awareness of their own thoughts and feelings, to assess if they are ready. The difference between nervous, excited curiosity with a partner who is loving and respectful, and acquiescence to intimacy that feels one-sided, can be the difference between the healthy beginning of adult sexuality and an experience that feels abusive and, sadly, may elicit shame.

Drugs and alcohol

Most parents want their teenager to avoid experimenting with alcohol or taking illicit drugs. Yet the chances that our teenagers and young adult children will be exposed to alcohol and drug use is almost guaranteed. If they decide to experiment, we are unlikely to be in a position to stop it. So where do we begin? We can start with an approach psychologists call 'harm minimization'. We recognize that we have less control than we would like (especially with older teenagers), and that the only control we *do* have is to remain a trusted advisor. This means maintaining open communication with our children (via empathic reflections), so they feel safe to disclose feelings, concerns and plans.

Similar to that *other* subject that parents would prefer to avoid (sex), our fear tends to steer us off course, so that we avoid discussions or over-emphasize the potential for disaster. In both cases, however, teenagers are better prepared to navigate the pull of drugs (or sexual activity before they are ready) if they have the full story.

Drugs and alcohol make many people feel temporarily ... good. Great, even. That's why drugs are so risky. If drugs didn't feel good, nobody would bother using them and addiction wouldn't be a concern. Arm your child with *all* the knowledge they need. Help them understand that the good feelings are a hidden trap — tricking the brain into wanting more and increasing the risk of addiction. That way, if they are being invited to try drugs — or indeed, are taking a drug for the first time — rather than thinking, 'Mum and Dad had no clue — this stuff is amazing!' they will more likely recognize the dangers: 'I'd better be careful, this good feeling is the red flag my parents told me about.'

Safety

There are many ways to increase safety for our teenagers. These can be summarized into three priorities. Each can be explicitly taught and modelled:

- Providing a safety net.
- Teaching teens to trust their instincts.
- Learning a language for 'no'.

Providing a safety net ... without question

We want our teenagers to know they can turn to us if they feel unsafe or in danger. The concept of 'without question' is one that encourages parents to explicitly state the message that they can contact you at *any time, for any reason, and in any state* (sober or otherwise).

This strategy frequently fails. Teenagers may have years of

experience telling them not to trust such a claim when their poor choice, lie or broken rule led to huge anger, judgement and disproportionate punishment.

Keep the consequences, remove the anger and judgement

So how do we make 'without question' a working plan, rather than wishful thinking? We are presented with an opportunity every time our child makes a mistake or breaks a rule. If your child is not yet a teenager, the mistakes will likely be small 'misdemeanours'; part of testing boundaries and learning impulse control.

By first listening, and then responding calmly and compassionately, you will help them learn important lessons — and keep yourself in the loop. Consider the example below, of a young girl telling a lie. Notice how her parent utilizes empathic reflections to help her build confidence in her ability to tell the truth.

> *Mia:* 'I want ice cream!'
> *Mum:* 'Mia, I know you'd like ice cream for dinner. Spaghetti is for dinner, then ice cream.'
> (Later …)
> *Mia:* 'I finished! Can I have dessert now?'
> *Mum:* 'Sure, here's your ice cream.'
> (Later still …)
> *Mia:* (crying) 'Mummy, I didn't really eat my dinner.'
> *Mum:* 'Hmm, sounds like you lied and that's made you feel sad.'
> *Mia:* (crying harder) 'I put it in the bin when

you were outside.'
Mum: 'You wish you'd made a different choice,
huh?'
Mia: 'Sorry Mummy.' (hugs).
Mum: 'Thank you for telling me the truth. I
know that can be hard sometimes.'

Mia felt sufficiently safe to acknowledge an impulse that she now
regrets. Encouraged by previous 'confessions' and their relatively
low-key outcomes, Mia blurts out the truth. It is very likely that
Mia will continue to tell her mother when she makes an impulsive choice. At this young age, those choices aren't likely to be
high-risk endeavours. But as Mia gets older and has more independence, risk increases.

Mia: 'Yay! Sleepover time! I can't wait!'
Mum: 'Great. Grab your bag and let's go!'
(Later, by telephone.)
Mia: 'Hey Mum? Can I come home? I'm not
feeling so good. '
(Later still, on the way home.)
Mum: 'So what's going on, Mia? You're not
well?'
Mia: 'No … it's not that. I just … I just didn't
like it there.'
Mum: 'Okay. Any idea why you didn't like it?'
Mia: 'The mum was yelling a lot. She had a
fight with this guy that was there.'
Mum: 'I'm sorry to hear that. You made a

really good choice to come home. You noticed
you were feeling uncomfortable, and you
knew you didn't have to stay there. I think you
should be really proud of yourself.'
Mia: 'Thanks Mum.'

Teenage Mia is now old enough to attend a sixteenth birthday
party, and someone has brought alcohol. With little or no experience, Mia drinks too much and becomes sick in the bathroom.
She is dizzy, embarrassed and a little scared about all the drunk
teenagers around her. She's also scared of the consequences but
recalls her parents' repeated mantra: *without question*. She texts
her dad, asking to be picked up. It's only 9 p.m., so he knows
something is up.

Dad: 'No problem, I'm on my way. Are you
okay?'
Mia: 'I don't feel good. Sorry, Dad.'
Dad: 'Okay. Let's talk about it later. I'm glad
you rang.'
Mia: 'Thanks.'
Dad: 'You'll be okay. Wait for me at the front
door.'
Mia: 'I've been drinking.'
Dad: 'I thought that might be the case. Let's
get you home. We'll work out the rest in the
morning.'

Over-the-top reactions to poor decisions teach teenagers to

hesitate before reaching out and confiding — even at the cost of their safety. Mia might have chosen to remain at the party in a vulnerable state. She might have tried to walk home by herself or accept a lift from someone without assessing their sobriety. As for consequences, when the storm (and hangover) has passed, and the message is conveyed with respect and calm, your teen is far more likely to accept a consequence with good grace. The consequence is to help your teen's brain connect the choice to its outcome. The message is 'I get it, you're still learning.'

Teaching children to trust their instincts

Children learning to tune inwards is the natural outcome of using empathic reflections. Mia's parents helped build this skill throughout her childhood. When Mia wanted to come home from a sleepover, her mother named the importance of trusting her instincts, saying, 'You noticed you were feeling uncomfortable.' This is further reinforced with empathy and encouragement. Trusting our instincts that something isn't quite right can also be taught explicitly.

> 'Now that you are allowed to go to the park without an adult Mia, I want to remind you of something. Most people you meet will be friendly, just having fun in the park too. But every now and then, you might see someone and feel uncomfortable. You might not even be sure why — but it is important to listen to your inner alarm bell. Trust it and come straight home.'

In theory, this should be sufficient. But children receive many messages that directly contradict this: always be polite; respect your elders; do what adults tell you to do. We can address this with slight changes and additions to these messages.

> 'Sometimes it is important to follow instructions from adults. But sometimes it is important to ignore them. Being safe is more important than being polite. Let's see how many examples we can come up with ...'

> 'It's okay to keep little secrets, like what we are buying Daddy for his birthday. But if someone asks you to keep a secret and you don't want to — there are two people you can *always* tell. That's your mummy and your daddy.'

A language for 'no'

Encourage your child, from as early as possible, to develop simple, specific phrases that clearly communicate 'no'. Your child might add slang, prefer humour or take the popular option of 'blaming' you! They might also be happy to use a blunt response that brooks no discussion. Whether your child is naturally assertive or will take time to develop the skill, help them get started, and acknowledge any attempt to be assertive that they share. Some examples are below:

> 'No thanks, not my thing.'
> 'It's a *no* from me!'
> 'Nope, not ready for that.'

'No way, my parents would kill me.'

'If I change my mind, I'll let you know.
Meanwhile please stop asking.'

'What I want for the next few years is a boy-
friend/girlfriend to hold hands and kiss.'

'Oh, that sounds like pressure to me. Not cool.'

'It's always a "no" when I'm not sober.'

'Ha! Your attempt to pressure me is noted!'

A final note: when to seek help

Your teenager's developing brain will not fully achieve matu-
rity until their mid-twenties. In typically developing teenagers,
mindful parenting can lessen the risks that come with growing
independence. Teenagers who know themselves well can assert
themselves, have practice assessing risks, and enjoy the confidence of a loving parent's safety net will transition more easily
from follower to independent thinker.

There are times however, when professional help is advisable
to support mental health. A decline in grades, signs of alcohol
or drug abuse, withdrawal from friends or favourite activities,
a change in eating habits, self-harm, references to hopelessness
and/or suicide, or an extended period of irritability, low mood or
anger are all indications that a teen may need additional support
(and this is not an exhaustive list). As always, the earliest possible
intervention is best, so please — trust your own observations and
instincts, and extend your safety net to include trusted profes-
sionals where necessary.

CHAPTER 12

Key mindfulness messages for parents

Angela North

Parents are busy people. If they were to speed-read this book, there are two messages that hopefully they would absorb before rushing off to feed an infant, make a school lunch or buy shoes for a teen's ever-growing feet.

The first of these is learning to listen. Most of us can hear, but how many of us are listening with the intent of gaining understanding, rather than gaining the upper hand? Sometimes we are so eager to share our own thoughts and solutions that we are simply waiting for our child to pause so we can get our Very Important Message across.

Genuine listening is not as passive as it sounds. We are focused, looking for clues — in body language, tone and words — to what our child is communicating. We are aware, recognizing and accepting our own thoughts and emotions as they appear, and setting them aside until the time is right. We are courageous, especially when we suspect the conversation is headed somewhere we don't want to go. We are compassionate, to ourselves and our child. Because children need to be heard and understood — and then they need us to get out of their way. They have their own path to forge, and it will look nothing like our own.

The second key message is the importance of setting boundaries with calm compassion. Just because our child is forging a different path, it doesn't mean they don't need guidance. When young children struggle with self-control, it is our willingness to step in and provide containment that provides them with emotional security. Parents who ignore behaviours or shy away from setting limits may be under the misconception that their love will be enough. Love is essential, of course. Sadly, however, it will not, on its own, teach a child healthy boundaries, social skills, confidence and resilience. Children without boundaries are like a small boat lost in a huge ocean. Behind their problematic behaviours you will find anxiety. Despite their sometimes-loud resistance, boundaries make children feel safe.

If you find empathic reflections or setting limits with calm compassion difficult, even after a great deal of practice, please seek professional guidance. Chances are that the generations before you were not able to pass on this gift. You can be the turning point for your family, giving the compassion and support you always needed, but perhaps did not receive. And then? You get to be the pebble that drops into the pond, sending out ripples of wisdom to your children and all the generations that follow. That can be a parent's legacy, and it's yours for the taking.

Stephen McKenzie

- Avoid over-reactions!
- Get out of the way of young people's natural mind-fulness and heartfulness.
- Keep an eye on our parenting ball by really listening to and seeing the needs and opportunities of the child. This is true for all children and especially for very young children without language, because they have no other way of communicating with us. Thankfully, we don't start off being parents of teen-agers, who can challenge us with complicated reasons for doing or not doing what we want them to do.
- Communicate deeply and honestly, even with some-one who can't yet talk back to us, or who never stops talking back to us! Real communication only hap-pens in this moment and it only happens with people who we are fully connected with, here and now.
- Attend fully to the reality of this moment. This allows us to respond to a very young person's subtle needs, as well as to their obvious ones, including for affir-mation, stimulation and relaxation.
- Let go of whatever we think we can't let go of, such as our resentment, anger and anxiety.
- Forgive!
- Come back to love. We can all be parenting were-wolves. We can all lose whatever is best about us, at least occasionally. We can all surprise ourselves and

others with our lack of humanity or true mindful-ness. We can also keep coming back to what is really important, no matter how far behind we think we have left it. We can all keep coming back to love.

- Never lose hope, and never lose love!

'If we learn to open our hearts, anyone, including the people who drive us crazy, can be our teacher.'
Pema Chōdrōn

PART 4

Resources

CHAPTER 13

Therapeutic play sessions: Recommended toy list

Angela North

The Center for Play Therapy at the University of North Texas is the largest play therapy training program in the world. Its founder Dr Garry Landreth is an internationally renowned play therapy expert and author. He once stated, 'Toys are used like words by children, and play is their language.'[1]

For this reason, the toy kit is carefully selected to ensure that your child has 'words' for *all* their feelings, wishes and wants. It is not essential to have all the items listed below, but a few from each category is important. Most of these items can be made or purchased at opportunity or discount shops. Where possible, choose second-hand toys: some children (and their parents!)

can be overly concerned about messing up or breaking a toy that looks shiny and new, and this will affect the way they play.

You will notice that the kit does not include board games, books or other toys that have a prescribed way of playing. The toy selection is designed to allow your child to express their own imagination and creativity. For the same reason, dolls, figurines and so forth should preferably not be characters from a movie or book, nor represent 'famous' characters. A Superman figure will tend to be utilized as a hero involved in brave deeds, while a nondescript male figure can be a father, friend, robber or indeed a hero who saves the day! Toys that are highly recommended for inclusion are denoted with an asterisk.

Family and nurturing toys

- A doll family — figurines of women, men, children and babies. Allow for a greater number than is the reality for your family.*
- House or box with some doll's furniture (can be a cardboard box divided into four sections).*
- Soft animal toys, such as a family of teddies, lions, monkeys, etc. (one set is sufficient).*
- A collection of animals, such as plastic dogs, fish, whales, elephants, etc.
- Baby doll.*
- Bottle, dummy, nappy and blanket for the doll.
- Blanket and pillow, e.g. large enough for your child to use for themselves.*
- Dress-ups. Can be a square scarf, fabric piece, bag,

hat, mask, rope or costume jewellery.*
- Cooking items, e.g. plates, cups, bowls, saucepan, spoon, chopsticks, etc.*
- Toy food.*

Expressive and construction toys

- Crayons or Textas with drawing paper.*
- Blackboard or whiteboard.*
- Blocks. *
- Playdough.
- Small tray/container filled half-way with dry rice or sand.*
- Small tray/container filled half-way with water.
- Toy telephones (e.g. two toy mobile phones).
- Mirror.
- Sticky tape and glue stick.
- Scissors (appropriate to your child's age).
- Magic wand.*
- Old newspaper.

Other multi-use toys

- Play money.*
- Cash register.
- Medical kit.*
- Cars, trucks, aeroplanes, emergency vehicles.*

Aggression-related toys

- Inflatable bop bag (the type that can be wrestled or hit and it bounces back).
- Dart guns (darts/caps removed). See note below.
- Plastic soldiers.
- Dinosaurs or other aggressive-looking animals.*
- Piece of rope. A skipping rope with handles cut off is ideal.*
- Foam bats or swords.*
- Bendable rubber knife.*
- Handcuffs (only the rubber 'slip on/off' type, or ones that do not require a key).*
- Hand puppets/toys such as a dragon, wolf, or other aggressive looking animals.

Note: Some parents will be reluctant to allow play with aggressive toys, thinking that this will encourage aggressive behaviours. However, research shows that children need to express feelings of aggression in their play in order to release them. This helps them manage their anger more appropriately at other times. We can ensure healthy boundaries throughout the play session, redirecting any physical aggression aimed at us to an appropriate alternative ('You're angry and you want to hit Mum, but I'm not for hitting. You can hit the pillow instead and pretend it's me.'). In this way, we teach children that their feelings are accepted, and we are helping them learn appropriate behavioural boundaries at the same time. Gun play is particularly popular, used by children to work through ideas of power, authority and control. However, if you are uncomfortable with the inclusion of toy guns, please feel free to omit them from your toy selection.

Training in Filial Therapy

Many of the strategies outlined in this book are key elements of Play Therapy. Filial Therapy is an offshoot of 'non-directive play therapy', offering parents a relatively brief training program (approximately ten one-hour sessions) that will enable them to run therapeutic play sessions at home. Training will maximize the benefits of special play time and is highly recommended if you have the capacity. If you are interested in exploring this approach further, a quick search online should identify training near you. Filial Therapy is also known as 'Child Parent Relationship Therapy'.

CHAPTER 14

Mindfulness games for young children

Stephen McKenzie

The proof of any pudding is in its practice. The next chapters of *Mindfulness at Play* present mindfulness activities for younger and older children that will bring to life what the earlier sections of the book have set the scene for.

This chapter presents 25 mindfulness-for-children practices. These activities are presented in the format of a universal children's learning system, i.e. fun!

These mindfulness games can be practised in any order, and any number of times, and will greatly help children, and their parents or carers, as well benefit from them by being fully aware, fully accepting, fully connected and fully alive.

This chapter of *Mindfulness at Play* will help children, and all of us, remember what we already naturally are — mindful, happy and free. It will help children, and all of us, develop immunity to modern mindless busy-ness and stress by building on what children do better than anybody — enjoy learning.

Act like an ape

Apes sometimes copy what other animals or people do — just for fun! 'Simon Says' is a children's game that was invented a long, long time ago, possibly by someone called Simon. Whoever invented the game might not have intended it to be a wonderful way of helping people pay full attention, and receive those benefits; however, that's what it is!

While most of us know how to play 'Simon Says', for those who don't it is essentially a game in which one person is the leader (Simon) and directs other people to say or do so something. Simon starts each order with the sentence: 'Simon says to …'

For example:
'Simon says — put your hands on your head!'
'Simon says — spell elephant!'

Everyone watches and listens carefully to what they do or say, and then does exactly the same thing.

Sometimes Simon will give an order that does not start with the sentence 'Simon says' and that means the others in the game do not follow the order.

The trick is to be listening and watching very carefully so as not to get confused between what is the real order and what is not.

Does watching and listening make the game more fun?
Does watching and listening help you do well at the game?

Buzz like a bee

This game helps us remember our natural state of full awareness by enabling us to recognise it first in ourselves and then in everything we do.

Bee still.
Feel a buzzing in your body.
Maybe it's in your toes.
Maybe it's in your nose.
It doesn't matter where it is.
Feel the buzzing growing stronger.
Feel the energy — the life in your body.
Feel it flow and grow!
Just allow the buzzing to bee … and bee stronger and stronger and stronger!

What was it like feeling your body buzzing like a bee?
What was it like to just bee?

Create like a magician

Giving our full attention to what's real, like the nose on our face or the rose in our garden, doesn't mean that we can't create, imagine and invent worlds of make believe. We can give all of our attention to what we have just made real, just as we can give all of our attention to what's already real.

Let's pretend that you are whoever and whatever you would like to be — right here, right now!

Let's pretend that a magic genie has magically appeared

— right here, right now!

The magic genie offers to turn you into whatever you would like to be.

You can be a pirate, a princess, a pony or a person that you like … or even a person that you don't like!

Let go of what you think you are.
Let go of what you usually are.
In this game you can be anybody at all.
In this game you can play any game.
In this game you can play with whoever you like …

Give your full attention to what you have created.
Give your full attention to what you have made real.

How did you go?
Was it fun letting go of what you usually are and creating something new?

Draw like an artist

Drawing is a wonderful way of being alert, attentive, calm and happy, because it helps us make connections: to what we're drawing, to what we're drawing with, to what we're drawing on, and to the act of drawing itself.

Find something fun to draw.
It might be something that looks beautiful, or it might be something that doesn't look beautiful — yet.

Really look at what you have chosen to draw — whether it's a person, or an animal, or a tree, or anything.

Then draw it very carefully.

Pay attention to the pencil or crayon or brush strokes on the paper as you draw.

What was it like drawing with full attention?
Was it fun?

Eat like an orangutan

Orangutans are apes that live in forests in places like Sumatra and they mainly eat fruit. The word orangutan means 'man of the forest' in the Indonesian language; however, these creatures never eat like people sometimes do, distracted by doing something else, such as watching television.

This game is a fresh food version of a well-known eating with attention experiment that often uses a sultana. This game teaches us that the proof of any pudding is in its eating. When we really give our attention to what we eat, it tastes nicer!

Find a grape.

If you can't find a grape, find another small piece of fresh fruit, such as a plum.

If you can't find a small piece of fruit, find a bigger piece of fruit, such as a mandarin.

If you can't find a bigger piece of fruit, find an enormous piece of fruit, such as a watermelon!

Give your full attention to the piece of fruit.
Really look at it.
Really smell it.
Really feel it.
Really taste it.

How good does the fruit taste when you give it your full attention? Now try it with other kinds of food and notice how much better everything is starting to taste!

Float like a butterfly

Floating is a wonderful way of letting go. We might think that if we are not actively swimming or struggling to keep our heads above the water we will go under, but we won't. We can let go of any of our ideas, such as our idea that we can't float, and just float.

The next time that you go swimming, don't swim for a moment.
Don't do anything … for a moment.
Let go of doing and just be … floating in the water.

Feel the water holding your body up.
Feel the peace of just bobbing up and down in the water like a cork.
Hear the sounds of the water swishing around you.

What did it feel like to let go of doing anything, and just float? Was it fun?

Give like a birthday cake

There are lots of old sayings that contain many elements of truth. One of these is that it is better to give than to receive. The best thing that we can give is our attention, because this gives life to everything we see and do.

Giving things to people makes *them* feel good.
Giving things to people makes *us* feel good.
Giving is fun!
Giving people presents makes them happy — not just because the presents are nice, but because we are nice, for giving them!

We can give people *presence* as well as *presents*.
We can give people our full attention.

Give your full attention to the next thing that you see.
Give your full attention to the next thing that you hear.
Give your full attention to the next person who talks to you.

What was it like giving your full attention?
What was it like giving the gift of your full attention to someone talking to you?
Was it fun for you?
Was it fun for them?

Huff like a horse and puff like a dragon

We can huff in happiness in a game of draughts when we take our opponents' piece. We can huff and puff, and blow people's houses down (or pretend to) like the wolf in the *Three Little Pigs* story. We can huff (and puff!) when we breathe, or we can huff and puff softly and quietly ... Being aware of our breathing can help bring us back to what's happening inside of us, no matter what's happening outside of us.

Take a great big breath in ...
and now huff it out like a horse or puff it out like a dragon!
Feel the air come in and go out.
Feel what happens in your body as the air comes in and goes out ...

Now take a tiny little breath in ...
and let it out very softly and gently ...
Feel the air come in and go out.
Feel what happens in your body as the air comes in and goes out ...

Now just breathe like you usually do.
Feel the air come in and go out.
Feel what happens in your body as the air comes in and goes out ...

What was it like being aware of your breath?
If you feel like too much is happening — inside your body or out-side it, just feel your breath — going in and coming out.

Joke like a jester

In the Middle Ages, jesters were people who entertained other people, usually kings and queens, by making light of things, even things that seemed very serious or sad. Jesters were good at making people laugh even when there didn't seem to be anything funny to laugh at. Jesters, clowns and our modern-day comedians are very useful people. Laughing is good for all of us, and seeing the joke can be the best thing of all for us to see …

You can see life's fun by smiling at it, or laughing at it, or with it. Think about something that makes you smile or laugh, then smile or laugh!
It might be a joke someone told you or that you made up.
It might be something funny that somebody said or did …

Now think about something that doesn't usually make you smile or laugh, then smile or laugh!
It might be something serious or even sad …
Is there something about what seems serious or sad that's just a little bit funny?
Maybe something seems to have gone so awfully hideously horribly wrong, like your team losing by a hundred goals, that you can see a funny side or a smiley side or another side of!

Now share your smile or laugh with someone else …

What does it feel like to smile or laugh?
Is it hard or easy?
What does it feel like to share your smile or laugh?

Is it hard or easy?

Does smiling and laughing make you feel good?

Does smiling and laughing make the person you smile or laugh with feel good?

Kill time like a Time Lord

Doctor Who was, is and will always be, a Time Lord. This means that time isn't the same for them as it is for most people because they can travel through it — they can see through it — they can find and keep any time. We can get stuck on times gone by and on times yet to come by thinking about them. However, just by focusing only on the time we are in right now, we can be timeless!

The next time someone asks you what time it is you could answer in several different ways:

'It's time you bought a watch!'

'It's lunch time!'

'It's too early!'

'It's too late!'

However, you could also pretend to be a Time Lord and say something even more interesting and true such as, 'The time is NOW!'

What was it like killing time and being timeless like a Time Lord? Was it fun?

When we realize that there is NO TIME, it's easy to LIKE THE PRESENT because that's really all there is.

Listen like a lynx

Listening is a wonderful way of giving our full attention.

Find a small bird.
If you can't find a small bird, such as a bell bird or a robin, find a bigger bird, such as a magpie or a parrot or a kookaburra.
If you can't find a bigger bird, find an enormous bird, such as an emu!
Give your full attention to the sound that the bird is making right here, right now!
Really listen to the bird.

How beautiful does the bird sound when you give it your full attention?
How beautiful does anything sound when you give it your full attention?

Move like a cat

Cats naturally move beautifully. Cats don't stumble or fumble — they are agile and sleek because they are inherently fully aware of their movements.

Find a way of moving that you enjoy.
This might be going for a walk,
or playing a sport,
or dancing,
or anything.

When you do anything that involves moving, give your full attention to the movement.
Really feel your body move.
Really feel your feet touching the ground.
Really feel the ball touching your hand.
Really feel the music …

What was being really aware of your movements like?
Was it fun?

Notice like a know-all

Sometimes things might happen at school or home that feel overwhelming. Although these things might happen around us, they can feel like they are happening inside of us and make us feel bad in some way. Feeling our body can bring us back from our worries of what has happened and what might happen into what's really happening right here and right now.

If things seem to be going wrong, you don't need to get upset or stay upset.
Just really notice what's happening — outside and inside you!

Stop!
Give your attention to something you can touch, such as your nose or ears.
Then touch it!

What was feeling your nose or ears like?

Was it more fun than getting upset?

Our noses and ears keep growing as we get older.
They never stop growing.
This means that it keeps getting easier to find them and feel them!

Observe like an owl

Acting like an owl can help us pay attention, because they are very good at being still and paying attention.

Be so still that you can watch your body.
Be so still that you can feel the sensations in your body coming, and going …
Be so still that you can feel the breath entering your body through your mouth or nose.
Be so still that you feel you can feel the breath leaving your body through your mouth or nose.
Be so still that you can watch your thoughts coming, and going …

What did it feel like to be still?
Was being still fun?
Did being really still help everything be fun?

Puzzle like a pyramid

The pyramids are enormous stone buildings in the Egyptian desert. One of them has a huge statue of a sphinx (body of a lion and the head of a human) built into the front of it. The sphinx is a puzzle because no one is quite sure who created it or why. It is also created a puzzle because it apparently guarded the entrance to the ancient Greek city of Thebes and asked a riddle of anyone who wanted to pass into the city. Puzzles are wonderful for mindfulness because we need to concentrate well to find a solution. Puzzles are also wonderful because we solve puzzles best when we stop puzzling!

Find a puzzle.
It can be puzzling to find a good puzzle to play with, because there are so many good ones.
Start puzzling by finding just one puzzle — then solve it!

Jigsaws are wonderful puzzles.
Jigsaws are called jigsaws because they can be made by sawing up a big bit of wood into lots of little bits of wood with a jigsaw! We can solve jigsaw puzzles just like we can solve lots of other puzzles — big and small — by putting their pieces together!
To put jigsaw puzzle pieces together we need to look very carefully at each piece and at how each piece fits into the big picture. When we put a jigsaw puzzle together, we get to enjoy a beautiful big picture.
We also get to enjoy each beautiful bit that makes up the big picture.
Overall, we enjoy the attention we need to solve them.

What was it like giving your full attention to a puzzle?
What was it like solving a puzzle?

Quantum leap like a quark

Leaping is fun because it takes us from one place to another one, very quickly! A quantum leap is a special leap we do with our minds, from one way of thinking to another one. A quark is a particle that's so small that no one's ever seen one. Everything in the universe is made up of quarks — from elephants to galaxies. We can quantum leap through our own bodies and find wonderful new feelings and ideas.

Things that we think are happening outside of us, such as earthquakes or someone talking to us, also happen inside of us in our bodies by the way they make us feel.

The next time that something uncomfortable happens in your body, quantum leap your attention to where it's happening.
Maybe there's an uncomfortable feeling in your tummy, chest, throat or face.
Once your attention has quantum leapt to where the uncomfortable feeling is, just be with it.
Just let it be!

What was it like just being with an uncomfortable feeling?
What was it like quantum leaping to wonderful new places, and spaces?

Receive like a radio

When we fine tune the static of our life, our life distortions, our life interference, we can clearly receive life.

When we listen to the radio, we can sometimes hear static if we haven't tuned into a station properly. Just like a radio, when we don't tune into ourselves properly, we can become distracted by our own form of static and can't hear clearly what our body is trying to tell us.

Tune into the next sound that you hear, without naming it, without thinking about it.
Really listen to the next sound that you hear that is close.
Now really listen to the next sound that you hear that is far away.
Be present to all the sounds that you receive.

Really listen to the next person who talks to you.
Really listen to the next sound that you hear …

Now tune in to the sounds of silence!
Rest in the space between the sound channels.
Enjoy the sounds of silence!

What was it like fine tuning into sounds?
What was it like fine tuning into silence?
Was tuning into sounds and silence fun?

Snap like a crocodile

Snap is a card game that's played by two or more players who divide a pack of cards up between them and then take turns putting down one of their cards face up in front of them, gradually building up a pile. A player calls out 'Snap!' when they put down a card that matches the one on top of the card pile. This game might not have been invented as an attention training activity, but that's what it is!

Give your full attention to each card being played in the snap game, not thinking about the *last* card, not thinking about the *next* card. Give your full attention to *this* card!

Does playing snap with full attention make the game more fun to play?
Does playing snap with full attention help other things you do be more fun?

Tell it like it really is

This game helps us pay attention to what's naturally interesting — everything — and then share information with others.

Look out for something interesting happening at your kindergarten, school or home.
Maybe it's your teacher saying something very clever.
Maybe it's your friend saying something very funny.
Maybe you will see, smell, hear, feel or taste something new.
Maybe you will see, smell, hear, feel or taste something wonderful.
Maybe you will feel glad or sad.
Maybe you will have an adventure!

Tell somebody about what happened.
Tell somebody about what you noticed.
Tell somebody exactly how it felt, smelt, sounded, looked, tasted.

Share your adventure!

What was it like looking out for interesting stories to report?
What was it like sharing your story?

Unite like a universe

Our universe is enormous, much bigger than our planet Earth, much bigger than our galaxy the Milky Way. Our universe is so big that everything we know, as well as everything we don't, is in it!

The word universe means 'combined into one'. We can read or write our own verses, or play our own parts, or do our own thing. However, our single verses sound best when we read them together, when we play together, when we work together … universally!

Read a poem with someone, or with a group (it doesn't matter what poem you read).

Play a musical instrument with someone, or with a group (it doesn't matter what musical instruments you play).

Play a game with someone, or with a group (it doesn't matter what game you play).

Play a play with someone, or with a group where each of you plays a part in the play (it doesn't matter which parts you play).

Dance with someone, or with a group (it doesn't matter what dance you dance).

Walk with someone, or with a group (it doesn't matter where you walk, or why).

Work with someone, or with a group (it doesn't matter what work you do).

What was it like reading a poem, playing, dancing, walking or working with someone, or with a group?
Was it fun?

View like a view finder

When we look into a camera's view finder, what we see can look sharp or it can look fuzzy. We can improve our view by adjusting the camera's focus until we can clearly see what we are looking at.

Look at something.
It doesn't matter what it is.
It might be an ant.
It might be an elephant.
It might be an elephant *on* an ant (not for very long!).
It might be your sister or brother or aunty or uncle …
It doesn't matter what it is.
Look at it very, very, very carefully!
Don't think about what you're looking at, don't think something like —
this is an ant, or an elephant, or an auntie …
Don't think anything about what you're looking at, like —
this is an angry ant, or elephant, or auntie!
Just look at it carefully, and calmly, and consciously …
Just allow it to be whatever it is, without thinking that it's anything else.
Focus on whatever you're looking at, until you see it clearly, until you see it —
as it is!

What was it like looking at something carefully, calmly and consciously?

Watch like a wave watcher

Surfers spend some of their time surfing, and most of their time watching the waves, waiting for a good one. It's the same with other sports — the better you watch, the better you play.

There was once a great Australian Rules football player called Peter Hudson. Peter was a great football player because he was a great football watcher. He watched the ball all the time, even when somebody kicked it up into the stands, even when he was waiting for the game to start again. He knew that when our attention wanders, we often drop the ball!

When you next play basketball, netball, volleyball, hockey, football or anything at all with a ball (or marble!), really watch the ball.

Don't watch your hands or other people's hands or your thoughts.

Just watch the ball …

How did you go?
Did you play the ball well when you really watched it?
Was it fun playing with the ball when you really watched it?

eXcel like a xylophone

We might think that excelling means getting excellent test results. It can also mean excelling in our connection with and enjoyment of what we are doing, whatever we are doing.

Making music is marvellous.
It's fun and it's natural to make sounds and melodies and rhythms.
They can make us, and other people, feel good.

Play some music just for fun.
You can play on a Xylophone, or a piano, or a triangle, or any-
thing!
If you get good at it — good!
If someone helps you get good at it — good!
Don't worry about playing well.
Don't worry about doing anything well.
Give full attention to playing music (or whatever you're doing).
Give full acceptance to playing music (or whatever you're doing).
Don't worry about the *results* of what you are doing.
Just do it!
Just feel it!

What did playing music with full attention feel like?

Yoga like a yogi

There was once a famous American cartoon bear called Yogi —
a fun-loving one. There was once a famous American baseball
coach called Yogi — a game-loving one. There are some not-
quite-so-famous people called yogis — who love fun and games.
Yogis do yoga and other fun things that help them be happy,
healthy and calm, and it's easy to be happy, healthy and calm

when you're having fun!

You don't have to stand on your head to do yoga (although you can if you want to!).
To do yoga you just have to pay full attention to how you move … and even to how you don't move!

Yoga has lots of great moves that are named after animals.
To do the cobra yoga move lie down on your tummy with your legs out straight behind you and your arms resting at your side.
Now slowly raise your body off the floor like a cobra!
Rest in the cobra position for a little while then do it again.

To do the cat yoga move, get down on your hands and knees.
Arch your back as you breathe out, then let your back right down as you breathe in.
Rest in the cat position for a little while, then do it again.

To do the lion yoga move, crouch down like a lion and look up with your eyes.
Then let out all the air in your body … with a ROAR!

How do you feel when you play the yoga game?
How do you feel when you give all your attention to your body —
moving or staying still?
Is it fun?

Zoom like a movie camera

Let your attention wander all over your body.
What's happening in your body right here and right now?
Really feel your body without thinking about it or judging it.

Now zoom your attention to your toes — really feel your toes ...
Now zoom to your feet — really feel them ....
Now your legs ...
Now zoom your attention to your tummy ...
Now your back ...

Now zoom your attention to your fingers — really feel your fingers ...
Now zoom to your hands — really feel them ...
Now your arms ...

Now zoom your attention to your neck, face and head — really feel each of them ...

Really feel whatever is happening in your body right here and now ...
Really feel your body as a whole and the peace that comes with accepting your body ... just as it is.

What was it like feeling your body?
Was feeling your body fun?

CHAPTER 15

Mindful stories for young children

Stephen McKenzie

Stories are a naturally wonderful way of giving children life lessons about the value of being mindful. Children naturally help bring these stories to life by willingly entering their wonderful world. The stories presented in this chapter bring to life the benefits of mindfulness for children described in earlier chapters.

1. Attention

A story about presence, and presents
(Inspired by Dr Seuss)

We can give children presents that plug into a wall or we can give them great stories, which answer their heart's call.
Whatever we offer, whatever we give —
sharing presents with presence is a great way to live!

*

There are mind cats that lurk in the minds of us all
that sneak into our paradise like a push before a fall.
When all seems *calm and quiet by day and by night*
our 'problems' are like bad dreams that can wake us in fright!
The answer to mind cats is not difficult, not slow —
if we stop damming our minds our mindfulness will flow!

*

Dr Seuss's snooty sneetches don't just live on beaches
and in books!
   They live in our fashions and judgmental looks!
   We're all of us equal, connected and free
even when we forget to remember to just be.
It might seem like fun to gloat, grin and boast
that we are the best sneetches living on the coast!
The best and worst sneetches are just ideas in our brain —
we're really all on the one great thought gravy train!

*

What is there left when we peel right away
the onion skins of who we think we are — by night and by day?
If we peel away our thought skins until all that we've got
is not what we think, *then we have not got a lot!*
When we haven't got a lot, then, as great life teachers say,
our nothing is everything, and our night is our day!
No matter how dull our life stories there's always light
 and endings that are eternally, wonderfully bright!

The present is a gift.

2. Resilience

Socrates was an Ancient Greek philosopher who was born in Athens in about 469 BC and died there roughly 70 years later. Socrates was executed by the state of Athens after a poisonous poet called Miletus brought a civil action against him for 'corrupting' the city's youth. In actual fact, he was teaching them to think for themselves. Before Socrates was forced to drink hemlock poison, he worked as a stone mason, soldier, teacher and philosopher. One of his students was Plato, an Ancient Greek playwright turned philosopher. Although Socrates wrote nothing, Plato gave the world Socrates's great life teachings in the form of plays.

Before he was executed, Socrates spent about a month chained in a prison cave. Socrates could see the Acropolis from his cave, the place where people gathered in large numbers to listen to him talk about how they could understand who they really were and how they could really be happy. Socrates's friends visited him in his cave prison every day and some of them wanted to bribe his jailor to let him out so that he could escape from Athens and live somewhere else. Socrates refused, and told his friends that it was his duty to do whatever the place he lived in and for wanted him to do, even if that was to be executed. Socrates knew so much about life that he wasn't scared of death, and died with courage, love and peace. One of his famous quotes about death is as follows:

'To fear death, gentlemen, is no other than to think oneself wise when one is not, to think one knows what one does not know. No one

201

knows whether death may not be the greatest of all blessings for a man, yet men fear it as if they knew that it is the greatest of evils.'

We can decide how we will respond, no matter what we are responding to.

3. Connectedness

A myth is a story that can be called true, not because the events in the story really happened but because they demonstrate a value or belief that we know to be true. King Midas was a famous mythic king who had been granted a special blessing that turned out to be an even greater curse. Everything King Midas touched turned to gold, which might sound pretty cool if you like gold, but what if you don't like eating gold food or drinking gold water? Hardly anybody knows about it but King Midas had an even more mythic sister, Queen Sadim. (This was a bit like the great fictional detective Sherlock Holmes having an even more fictional, and even more clever, brother called Mycroft.)

Sadim is Midas spelt backwards, and Queen Sadim had a very different outlook on life than her brother. Although they grew up in the same palace, with the same parents, the same servants, and went to the same school — Kingdom High — for some reason they turned out completely differently. While King Midas became greedier and greedier until all he wanted was gold, Queen Sadim had a different destiny.

One glittering morning on her way to work, in the throne room of the palace of her Queendom (which was right next door to King Midas's Kingdom) Queen Sadim decided that something was wrong. She realized that most people she knew wanted what her brother Midas wanted — gold. Queen Sadim also realized that most people were miserable because gold wasn't what they needed, or even really wanted. Queen Sadim understood that gold doesn't really make us happy. What really makes us happy is being really connected with other people.

It's not really all that clear how King Midas developed his mythic power of turning everything he touched into gold. We do know, however, how Queen Sadim developed her even more mythic power of turning everything she came into contact with into feelings of happiness. Queen Sadim totally connected with everything she touched, smelt, tasted, looked at and listened to. Queen Sadim simply allowed everything she came into contact with to be what it was, and she didn't want it to be what it wasn't.

In no time at all, Queen Sadim developed a power that was much more useful than the power of turning everything into gold. In no time at all, she felt a great connection to everything and everyone. Queen Sadim was happy, calm, kind and free, and she inspired the other people in her Queendom to be likewise.

We can learn from Queen Sadim that if we really connect with what we love or can love, we can create our own happiness.

4. Fun

Seeing the funny side

(Adapted from a story told to the author by Karl Haase.)

A mindfulness book writer decided one morning that he could

be a lot more mindful than he was, so he mindfully drove off up a mountain to a monastery. In this particular monastery you are only allowed to say two words a year, because talking too much can make us mindless.

After his first year in the mountain monastery, the mindfulness book writer said his first two words to the head monk.

'More food!'

After his second year in the mountain monastery, the mindfulness book writer said his second two words to the head monk.

'More blankets!'

After his third year in the mountain monastery, the mindfulness book writer said his third two words to the head monk.

'I quit!'

The head monk replied, 'Good, you've done nothing but complain ever since you arrived here!'

We don't need to take life too seriously!

5. Mindfulness

Monty was a wonderfully ordinary boy, who loved his wonderfully ordinary life with his family, his friends and his sausage dog, Max, in downtown Manangatang. Monty loved playing with his toys, especially the fast ones, and he loved his parents, Dallas and Dan, *especially* when they came home from work!

One drizzly September morning Monty woke up to a surprise. At the end of his racing car bed sat something that glittered and glowed bright red — a computer tablet! He turned it on quickly. Purple and red tablet people played — with each other! Monty was soon completely absorbed by his new tablet. The people inside it seemed more interesting, more captivating and more real than the people outside it.

A month later, on a Monday, Monty's teacher phoned his mother.

'Monty isn't paying attention at school,' said Miss Sharp crossly. 'He needs to do better!'

'You need to better!' said Monty's mother after school.

'We've put you in the best school in Manangatang!' said Monty's father. 'Why aren't you successful?'

On Tuesday Monty thought hard. How could he do better? How could he be successful? He thought and he thought and he ... thought! The more Monty thought the more he couldn't think ... of an answer!

On Wednesday night Monty had a dream. His purple and red computer tablet people grew and grew and grew — until out of their computer they flew — and zoomed into the school playground! They wouldn't play with Monty but only each other!

On Thursday Monty turned into a selfish monster. He wouldn't give Edgar's crocodile snap cards back after the game. He wouldn't return smiles to the other children. He wouldn't pay attention to Miss Sharp. Monty was even more selfish than his classmate Belinda — who wouldn't share anything with anybody — not even her germs!

On the weekend Monty turned into a TV monster. He watched even more television than TV Tess did. TV Tess watched television while eating TV dinners and TV breakfasts and even TV afternoon teas!

On Monday it rained and it rained and it rained and it ... rained! Monty wondered if he would have to swim to school because the streets were sooooo wet! At school the children huddled together in the shelter shed telling stories. Suddenly, Monty turned into a shark monster! He chased the other children out into the rain and yelled, 'Hey, look at me!'

Miss Sharp reigned him in quickly: 'MONTY, STOP BEING A MONSTER!'

Monty didn't like being yelled at. He didn't know what to do.

On Tuesday Monty snatched Miranda's birthday present book. It had wonderful pictures of happy children, even ones eating Brussels sprouts, and worse! Monty put down the book and said to Miranda, 'How can I be happy like the children in your book? I'm tired of being a monster!'

'It's easy to be happy!' Miranda told Monty. 'Just give all of your attention to everything you do — at home and at school and you will be present and cool! It's like when we play snap — we do our best when we enjoy ourselves most — just by paying attention to the next card!'

Monty remembered how good it felt to pay attention and decided he didn't want to be a monster anymore. He could just 'be'. Monty gave himself to life, and life gave itself to him. Monty's world began to light up again — from the inside — and he glowed like a shining star. Now Monty was happy just being Monty!

All we need to be happy is to just be who we really are, and stop creating mind monsters — unhelpful ideas about who we think we are.

CHAPTER 16

Living games, practices and experiments for older children and teenagers

Stephen McKenzie

Life can be a challenge. It doesn't have to be so challenging, however, that we can't enjoy it. When we are really mindful we live naturally, and this means that we give ourselves the opportunity to enjoy what whatever we are doing and be fulfilled by it. This chapter provides ways for teenagers to develop mindfulness and gain mindfulness benefits, and for parents and carers to help them do this. When you are giving or doing the activities presented in this chapter, just enjoy them without thinking about how well they are being done, or why they are being done. Doing the activities in this chapter will help all life activities feel really rewarding.

1. Be free of the results of your actions

Start by letting go of thoughts that can get in the way of the natural enjoyment of your activities such as:

> **Am I doing it right?**
> **Am I doing it as well as I should?**
> **Am I doing it as well as someone else is doing it?**
> **What's next?**

Any life activity is naturally enjoyable when we are so connected with it, we're not doing something else in our minds. Activities work best when we're not doing them because we think they might lead to some future gain, like success. When we let go of wanting to do things as a means to an end — which really means living our lives as a means to an end — we are free to be ... anything!

Try it now. Whatever activity you do next, do it with full acceptance, with full connection, and with full opportunity to really enjoy it.

2. Be free of your decisions

Start by letting go of any ideas that you have about what you should do next, and why, such as:

Is this what I should be doing?

Shouldn't I be doing something else or doing it with someone else?

The more we think about anything we think we need to do, the less we experience it and the more likely we are to make mistakes. The more we think, the less we live. Most of us mindlessly build up thinking patterns throughout our lives that separate us from what we do, from who we do it with, and from our natural enjoyment of our life activities. We don't need to decide what we should do; we can feel what we need to do.

Try it now. Whatever decision you make next, make it without thinking too much about it. Just be aware of your challenges and opportunities, and allow, rather than force, your best and most natural response.

3. Be timeless

Start by realizing that this time is all time.

We don't always need to rush to wherever we are going or whatever we are doing. We often think that we don't have enough time for peace, or enjoyment, or fulfilment. Do we have time for life?

Feel the stillness, in everything that you do or don't do. Allow yourself to feel eternity by entering a time oasis. Don't hurry, because you already are where you are, right here and right now.

Feel the infinite — timelessness — in everything that you do or don't do. Feel it even and especially in your mind-made busy-ness.

'That is the way to learn the most, that when you are doing something with such enjoyment that you don't notice that the time passes.'

Albert Einstein, in a letter to his eleven-year-old son, Hans Albert.

4. Be connected – through a living artwork

Start by helping your life be a great work of art by producing a mindful artwork.

There are many popular art-of-mindfulness activities available such as colouring in mindfulness-based picture books. These modern activities actually originated in ancient living art practices such as creating mandalas, illuminated writing and calligraphy. These practices help still the mind and open the heart. You can create a mindful life artwork right here and right now.

Step 1: **Draw or paint a picture, it doesn't matter what of.**

Step 2: **Really connect with the idea that we don't have to finish what we are doing — fast — so that we can do what's more important — whatever comes next! Nothing really comes next, because all that we have, and all that we need, is here in the moment now. Really feel the pen, pencil or paintbrush in your hand; feel the impact that it makes on the page; see what it is creating. Feel what you are doing and what it's like to be doing it, without thinking about it. Get out of the way of what you are** doing by not thinking about it. Just do it. Fully connect with the point where your pen, or pencil or other art instrument connects with its object — its meeting point, its turning point. This can help you transform a mental picture of what you think you are into a real picture of who you really are.

Step 3: Fully explore and share what you have created, and the experience of creating it.

5. Let your life tools work *for* you, not *against* you

Start by really feeling whatever tool you are using to express yourself, now. This might be a paint brush, or a pencil, or even a computer keypad.

It can seem like we are spending our lifetime in much the same way we try to escape from quicksand — the harder we try, the faster we sink. The difference between wrestling with life and dancing with life is the difference between struggling and allowing. We can practise allowing life to work for us and not against us by allowing …

- our pen or pencil to flow when we produce a picture
- our hands to flow when we are washing dishes
- our words to flow when we are having a conversation.

Try just allowing your life tools to work for you.

6. Move, from stillness to stillness

Start by connecting with the stillness at the heart of every activity.

This is the eye of the storm. Realize that everything moves from stillness to stillness — the waves of the sea, the words of a song, the breaths in our bodies, the thoughts in our minds, the days of our lives. When we realize that everything ends up where it started, we understand that the heart of any movement is the still point in the middle of the moving circle. We then realize the silent source of peace, happiness and creativity.

Whatever you do next, no matter what it is, experience the stillness at the heart of the activity, just as the centre of a moving wheel doesn't move.

7. Focus

Start by listening to the sounds you can hear, and not to the general noise.

Whether we experience life's noise or individual sounds depends on whether we focus on the reality of what is, such as what someone is actually saying, or get distracted by what isn't, such as what we think they are saying.

Really focus on whatever you hear next. If thoughts come into your mind let them come, let them go, and then bring your full focus back to what you are actually hearing. Don't think it; listen to it, connect with it, allow it.

Giving the full force of our attention to whatever we are hearing, right here and right now, and accepting the reality of whatever we are tuned into, right here and right now, gives our lives clarity.

8. Grow with the flow

Start by allowing yourself to be creative, and not dam your natural creative flow with ideas that you can't …

Great musicians like Mozart and Bach, great scientists like Newton and Einstein, great sportspeople like Shane Gould and Roger Federer, great artists like Michelangelo and Rembrandt, and great life artists like Mahatma Gandhi, Mother Teresa and Nelson Mandela didn't really *do* their great composing or thinking or performing or living. They allowed it to be done *through* them. They tuned into something greater than their idea of themselves and their limitations, so they became something greater than their idea of themselves and their limitations. Great musicians, scientists, sportspeople, artists and life artists enter a zone when allowing life to flow through whatever they are doing, rather than damming it with their ideas.

Be still and reflect on what you would like to create in your life. Get out of its way.

Create your own flow by selecting what you want to create and letting go of everything else. Try creating a nice mood by selecting one from all the many moods in your mind. Try creating a nice experience by selecting one from all the many experiences that are possible.

When you next do something, remember that you are really a great life *creator*.

9. Mindful study

Start by letting go of any unhelpful ideas that you might have about study such as:

I'm not good at study.
There are too many distractions for me to
study effectively.
I would rather be doing something else, any-
thing else!

Anyone can study effectively because everyone can practise mindfulness effectively. To study effectively, just don't do anything other than study. This means not being distracted by thoughts that might seem more interesting than what you are studying. These are really just our mind's attempts to sabotage our efforts. Minds like to be distracted, they like to zoom off in any direction other than the one that we are currently headed, such as by saying things like: 'Hey, this thought is really interesting, really important, why don't you drop your book or your laptop and climb aboard my thought train!'

Studying mindfully simply means giving our full attention to whatever we are studying, now, and creating study conditions that help us do this, such as by removing distractions.

Studying mindfully produces much better results. Doing less can actually result in achieving more, and help us increase our study quality rather than quantity.

Natural benefits of studying mindfully include:

- Increasing our 'growth mindset' (by developing our study skills over time, we start to believe we can do it), and decrease the 'fixed mindset' (for example, thoughts of 'I can't do it!').
- Increasing our deep learning. This is based on deep

knowledge of who we really are and what we really want — and makes study more effective because we are studying what we are genuinely motivated to study.

- Reducing our multi-tasking. We might think that we can effectively do more than one thing but that's an illusion. Mindfulness is based on the principle that we can really only fully give our attention to, and therefore do, one thing at a time.

10. Life experiments

Start by reflecting on what you would like to discover.

There have been lots of interesting scientific experiments that have led to interesting discoveries. But it's not just scientists who can make interesting discoveries, or conduct interesting experiments.

Reflect on something you would like to discover and how you can create an experiment that will help you find out what you want to know.

Most great scientific discoveries started with the premise of asking a question, which leads to another question and so forth.

Some interesting scientific research questions that have been previously asked include that by late nineteenth-century scientist Marie Curie. In 1903 Marie Curie saw a possible connection between the discovery of uranium rays and the beginnings of the X-ray. Researching this connection further brought about her groundbreaking theory of radioactivity and her first Nobel Prize. In 1911 Marie Curie's questioning led her to discover the

elements radium and polonium, and the use of radioactive iso-
types, both crucial to the development and advancement of the
modern X-ray machines and medical treatments. This led to her
second Nobel Prize.

In 1984, a 36-year-old medical researcher named Elizabeth
Blackburn, who was Australian by birth, co-discovered telomer-
ase, an enzyme that replenishes our telomeres, genetic structures
which protect the end of our chromosomes from DNA damage.
She did this after asking research questions including, 'What pro-
cesses are involved in ageing, and can these be sped up or slowed
down by stress?' In 2009 Elizabeth Blackburn was awarded the
Nobel Prize for Physiology. This work is particularly relevant to
the study of mindfulness, which has been showed to decrease
our rate of cellular ageing by reducing stress within our bodies.[1]

In another mindfulness-related scientific discovery, psychological researchers studying perception asked a question in the
1990s about whether we really pay attention to everything, all
the time, or whether we don't. These researchers ingeniously created an experiment in which they asked the participants to watch
a basketball game and count the passes thrown by each team.
What they didn't tell the participants was that some gorillas (or
actually people dressed as gorillas), would shoot in and out of the
game. As they were all focused on the passing of the ball, none of
the participants noticed![2]

Now it's time for you to create your own living experiments!

1. **Think of a research question that will help
    you discover something you have been
    curious about.**

2. Think of a method that will allow you to answer your research question.

3. Conduct your experiment.

4. Consider and share what you have learned.

11. The great game (of reason)

Rudyard Kipling's *Kim* is a story about the adventures of a British teenager who lived in India in the late nineteenth century, mostly happily, with no family and only a billion or so local Indians for company. In this story Kipling makes reference to the 'Great Game' which was an often deadly serious spying game played by British and Russian agents. The great game that's presented here, however, is a game of reasoning.

When we are mindful, we have a greater ability to use reason and thus it's easier for us to act reasonably. When we are reasonable, we can see reasons for why people have done things or behaved a certain way, which can help us to not become angry or upset with them.

You can play the great game (of reason) by yourself, or with a friend, or even with an enemy.

> *Step 1.* Think of someone who you don't like or even hate. The person can be someone you know, or someone you know about, or someone that other people have told you about. They might be alive or dead. They might be famous, or notorious, or completely unknown. It doesn't matter who they are.

Step 2. Think of why you don't like them. What have they done? Who have they done it to?

Step 3. Think about how it feels to not like them or hate them.

Step 4. Stop thinking and start reasoning.

Step 5. Consider reasons why the person did what they did to make you have such strong feelings about them. If you can't come up with definite reasons you can speculate. Does the person have a different point of view? Does the person have a physical or psychological problem that you don't know about?

Step 6. Consider *what you would do if you were in that person's shoes.* What would *you* have done? How would *you* feel?

Step 7. What and who do you feel like now?

References

Chapter 1

1. '*Scientifically supported benefits of mindfulness include …*' adapted from McKenzie, S., & Hassed, C. (2012, 2013). *Mindfulness for Life*, Exisle, Wollombi.

Chapter 2

1. '*Mindfulness is a skill that can easily be, and should be, taught …*' McKenzie, S., & Hassed, C. (2012). *Mindfulness for Life*, Exisle, Wollombi.
2. '*The reasons why teenagers do what they do include neurophysiological reasons …*' Dumontheil, I. (2016). 'Adolescent brain development.' *Current Opinion in Behavioral Sciences,* Vol. 10, Pages 39–44, ISSN 2352-1546, https://doi.org/10.1016/j.cobeha.2016.04.012.
3. '*In* A New Earth, *Eckhart Tolle …*' Tolle, E. (2016). *A New Earth: Create a better life.* Penguin Books, London, UK.

Chapter 3

1. '*Indeed, this inner voice can become a 'valuable self-regulation and motivational tool …*' Alderson-Day, B., & Fernyhough, C. (2015). 'Inner speech: development, cognitive functions, phenomenology, and neurobiology.' *Psychological Bulletin*, 141(5), 931–65. doi: 10.1037/bul0000021.
2. '*According to a recent review of mindful parenting outcomes …*' Ahemaitijiang, N. Fang, H., Ren, Y., Han, Z.R., & Singh, N.N. (2021). 'A review of mindful parenting: Theory, measurement, correlates, and outcomes.' *Journal of Pacific Rim Psychology*. Doi:10.1177/18344909211037016.
3. '*Research into the benefits of mindfulness for families is considerable, showing significant changes for children and adolescents …*' Ahemaitijiang, N., Fang, H., Ren, Y., Han, Z.R., & Singh, N.N. (2021). 'A review of mindful parenting: Theory, measurement, correlates, and outcomes.' *Journal of Pacific Rim Psychology*. Doi:10.1177/18344909211037016.
4. '*As Cline and Fay wrote …*' Cline, F., & Fay, J. (1990). *Parenting with*

Love and Logic, NavPress Publishing Group.

Chapter 4

1 *'Not being able to give and direct our full attention ...'* McKenzie, S. (2013). *Mindfulness at Work*, Exisle, Wollombi. (2014) Career Press, New Jersey.

2. *'An article published in the Harvard Business Review referred to hyper-kinetic workplaces ...'* Hallowell, E.M. (2005). 'Overloaded circuits: Why smart people underperform.' *Harvard Business Review,* January; 83(1), 54–62, 116.

3 *'A meta-analysis of the results of ten studies conducted by Molly Cairncross ...'* Cairncross, M., & Miller, C.J. (2020). 'The Effectiveness of Mindfulness-Based Therapies for ADHD: A Meta-Analytic Review.' *Journal of Attention Disorders*, 24(5), 627–643. https://doi.org/10.1177/1087054715625301.

4. *'If we do this in a driving simulator our driving is impaired as much as if we had a .08 blood alcohol reading ...'* Strayer, D.L., Drews, F.A., & Crouch, D.J. (2006). 'A comparison of the cell phone driver and the drunk driver.' *Human Factors*, 48(2), 381–391. https://doi.org/10.1518/001872006777724471.

5. *'Attention-switching (giving our full attention to only one thing at a time) ...'* Slagter, H.A., Lutz, A., Greischar, L., et al. (2007). 'Mental training affects distribution of limited brain resources.' *PLOS Biology*, June 2007;5(6):e138. doi:10.

6. *'A recent study of the effects on young people watching two screens ...'* Srisinghasongkram, P., Trairatvorakul, P., Maes, M., et al. (2021). 'Effect of early screen media multi-tasking on behavioural problems in school-age children.' *European Child Adolescent Psychiatry.*, 30, 1281–1297 (2021). https://doi.org/10.1007/s00787-020-01623-3.

7. *'A study by clinical psychologist Saskia van der Oord and colleagues in Belgium ...'* van der Oord, S., Bogels, S., & Peijnenburg, D. (2012). 'The Effectiveness of Mindfulness Training for Children and Adolescents with ADHD and Mindful Parenting for their Parents.' *Journal of Child Family Studies.*, 21:139–147.

8. *'Another study by Eva van de Weijer-Bergsma and colleagues ...'* van

de Weijer-Bergsma, E., Formsma, A., de Bruin, A., Bogels, S. (2012). 'The Effectiveness of Mindfulness Training on Behavioral Problems and Attentional Functioning in Adolescents with ADHD.' *Journal of Child Family Studies.*, 21, 775–787.

9. '*Mindfulness has been shown to significantly improve performance ...*' Dretzin, R., & Rushkoff, D. (2010). 'digital_nation life on the virtual frontier', *pbs.org Frontline*, February.

10. '*This stabilises attention and results in improved ...*' Dretzin, R., & Rushkoff, D., (2010). 'digital_nation life on the virtual frontier', *pbs.org Frontline*, February.

11. '*Spending more time communicating face to face rather than texting. This has been shown to reduce distractibility ...*' Levine, L.E., Waite, B.M., & Bowman, L.L. (2007). 'Electronic Media Use, Reading, and Academic Distractibility in College Youth.' *Cyber Psychology & Behavior*, Vol. 10, Issue 4 August.

12. '*Learning difficulties appear to be getting more common and there has been debate about whether this ...*' Hallahan, D. (1992). 'Some thoughts on why the prevalence of learning disabilities has increased.' *Journal of Learning Disabilities*, Vol. 25(8), Oct., pp. 523–528.

13. '*There is clear evidence that learning difficulties ...*' Sauer, S., Walach, H., Schmidt, S., Hinterberger, T., Horan, M., & Kohls, N. (2011). 'Implicit and explicit emotional behavior and mindfulness.' *Conscious. Cognition.*, 20, 1558–1569.

14. '*A study by Beauchemin and colleagues ...*' Beauchemin J.; Hutchins T.L., & Patterson F. (2008). 'Mindfulness meditation may lessen anxiety, promote social skills, and improve academic performance among adolescents with learning disabilities.' *Complementary Health Practice Review*, Jan; 13 (1): 34-45.

15. '*Another study found that mindfulness decreases ...*' Sauer, S., Walach, H., Schmidt, S., Hinterberger, T., Horan, M., & Kohls, N. (2011). 'Implicit and explicit emotional behavior and mindfulness.' *Conscious. Cognition.*, 20, 1558–1569.

16. '*Importantly, recent studies have shown that parents can administer mindfulness programs ...*' Guenther C.H., Stephens R.L., Ratliff M.L., & Short S.J. (2021). 'Parent-Child Mindfulness-Based Training: A Feasibility

and Acceptability Study.' *Journal of Evidence Based Integrated Medicine.* 2021 Jan–Dec;26:2515690X211002145. doi: 10.1177/2515690X211002145. PMID: 33896225; PMCID: PMC8082986.

17. '*Mrazek and colleagues, for example, showed that ...*' Mrazek, M., Franklin, M., Phillips, D., Baird, B., & Schooler, J. (2013). 'Mindfulness training enhances cognitive functioning and reduces mind wandering.' *Clinician's Research Digest: Child and Adolescent Populations,* 31(7)., pp. 3.

18. '*A large meta-analytic study of the emotional and social benefits of mindfulness ...*' Zenner, C. Herrnleben-Kurz, S., & Walach, H. (2014). 'Mindfulness-based interventions in schools—a systematic review and meta-analysis.' *Frontiers in Psychology,* Vol 5.

19. '*It does this by helping them regulate attention, deal with emotions, manage frustration and increase self-motivation ...*' mLearn (2012). Mobile and contextual learning, proceedings from the 11th World Conference on Mobile and Contextual Learning, Helsinki.

20. '*As Adele Diamond, professor of neuroscience at the University of British Columbia, nicely puts it ...*' Diamond, A. (2010). 'The evidence base for improving school outcomes by addressing the whole child and by addressing skills and attitudes, not just content.' *Early Education and Development.,* 21, 780–793, p789.

Chapter 5
1. '*The study was conducted in Germany and analysed the results of 24 scientific studies ...*' Zenner, C. Herrnleben-Kurz, S., & Walach, H. (2014). 'Mindfulness-based interventions in schools—a systematic review and meta-analysis'. *Frontiers in Psychology,* Vol 5.

2. '*Scientific studies using Mindfulness Behavioural Interventions (MBIs) ...*' Joyce, A., Etty-Leal, J., Zazryn, T., & Hamilton, A. (2010). 'Exploring a mindfulness meditation program on the mental health of upper primary children and adolescents: A pilot study'. Adv. Sch. *Mental Health Promotion.,* 3, 17–25.

Fjorback, L.O., Arendt, M., Ornbøl, E., Fink, P., & Walach, H. (2011). 'Mindfulness-based stress reduction and mindfulness-based cognitive therapy: A systematic review of randomized controlled trials.' *Acta Psychiatrica Scandinavia.,* 124, 102–119.

3. 'Scientific studies have also shown that mindfulness helps children and adolescents by ...' Sibinga, E.M.S., Kerrigan, D., Stewart, M., Johnson, K., Magyari, T., & Ellen, J.M. (2011). 'Mindfulness-based stress reduction for urban youth.' Journal of Alternative and Complementary Medicine., 17, 213–218.

Durlak, J.A., Weissberg, R.P., Dymnicki, A.B., Taylor, R.D., & Schellinger, K.B. (2011). 'The impact of enhancing students' social and emotional learning: A meta-analysis of school-based universal interventions.' Child Development., 82, 405–432.

4. 'For example, a meta-analysis conducted in 2016 showed that there was an overall positive ...' Lebuda, I., Zabelina, D.L., & Karwowski, M. (2016). 'Mind full of ideas: A meta-analysis of the mindfulness–creativity link.' Personality and Individual Differences, 93, 22–26.

5. '... an increased ability to switch perspectives ...' Langer, E.J. (2014). Mindfulness. Da Capo Press, Cambridge MA.

6. '...an increased ability to respond in a non-habitual fashion ...' Moore, A., & Malinowski, P. (2009). 'Meditation, mindfulness, and cognitive flexibility.' Consciousness and Cognition, 18, 176–186.

7. '... a reduction in people's fear of judgement ...' Carson, S.H., & Langer, E.J. (2006). 'Mindfulness and self-acceptance.' Journal of Rational Emotive & Cognitive-Behavior Therapy, 24, 29–43.

8. 'A systematic review of research studies on the relationship between mindfulness and creativity ...' Henriksen, D., Richardson, C., & Shack, K. (2020). 'Mindfulness and creativity: Implications for thinking and learning.' Thinking Skills and Creativity., Volume 37.

9. 'For example, a study showed that mindfulness improves divergent and also convergent thinking ability ...' Colzato, L.S., Ozturk, A., & Hommel, B. (2012). 'Meditate to create: The impact of focused attention and open-monitoring training on convergent and divergent thinking.' Frontiers in Psychology, 3, 116.

Chapter 6

1. 'There is ample evidence that humans behave in the same way.' Sharpe, L. (2011). 'So you think you know why animals play'. Scientific American (blog). https://blogs.scientificamerican.com/guest-blog/

so-you-think-you-know-why-animals-play/.

2. '*... children deliberately trigger 'fight or flight' responses ...*' Gray, P. (2019). 'Evolutionary functions of play: Practice, resilience, innovation, and cooperation.' In P. K. Smith & J. L. Roopnarine (Eds.), *The Cambridge handbook of play: Developmental and disciplinary perspectives* (pp. 84–102). Cambridge University Press.

3. '*These are the 'ghosts in the nursery', a metaphor introduced by social worker and psychoanalyst Selma Fraiberg ...*' Fraiberg, S., Adelson, E., & Shapiro, V. (1975). 'Ghosts in the nursery: A psychoanalytic approach to the problems of impaired infant-mother relationships.' *Journal of American Academy of Child Psychiatry*, 14(3), 387–421. https://www.sas.upenn.edu/~cavitch/pdf-library/Fraiberg_Ghosts.pdf.

Chapter 7

1. '*In fact, this ability to recognise our own (and others') emotions is a foundation of emotional intelligence ...*' Goleman, D. (1995). *Emotional intelligence. Why it can matter more than IQ.* Bantam Books, New York. Freedman, J., & Fariselli, L. (2016). *Emotional intelligence and success* [White paper]. 'Six seconds. The emotional intelligence network.' https://rw360.org/wp-content/uploads/2016/03/Six-Seconds-EQ-and-Success-White-Paper.pdf

2. '*As Gary Chapman, author of* Love as a Way of Life ...' Chapman, G. (2009). *Love as a Way of Life.* Doubleday, New York.

3. '*Once the plane was airborne, she turned to her mother...*' Glass, I., & Goldman, E. (2016, December 16). Kid Logic. [Radio broadcast transcript]. *This American Life.* https://www.thisamericanlife.org/605/transcript.

Chapter 8

1. '*Indeed, this approach has since been described as a 'quasi-religious con'.*' Storr, W. (2017, June 3). '"It was quasi-religious": The great self-esteem con.' *The Guardian.* https://www.theguardian.com/lifeandstyle/2017/jun/03/quasi-religious-great-self-esteem-con.

2. '*Self-esteem is great, it seems, if it is based in reality.*' Reville, W. (2018, November 15). 'Self-esteem is great – so long as it is rooted in reality.'

The Irish Times. https://www.irishtimes.com/news/science/self-esteem-is-great-so-long-as-it-is-rooted-in-reality-1.3692374.

Chapter 9

1. *'Critics challenged the idea that parents could make a difference in this way.'* VanFleet, R. (2011). 'Filial Therapy: What every play therapist should know.' *Play Therapy: Magazine of the British Association of Play Therapists.*, 66, 7–10. http://www.play-therapy.com/images_prof/FT.part2of3.BAPT.pdf.

2. *'Research across cultures, different family structures and behavioural problems …'* Lin, Y.W. & Bratton, S.C. (2015). 'A meta-analytic review of child-centered play therapy approaches.' *Journal of Counseling & Development*, 93(1), 45–58. http://dx.doi.org/10.1002/j.1556-6676.2015.00180.x.

3. *'Some research demonstrates that in comparison to trained play therapists, parents who utilise Filial Therapy can be even more effective …'* Cornett, N., & Bratton, S.C. (2014). 'Examining the impact of child parent relationship therapy (CPRT) on family functioning.' *Journal of Marital and Family Therapy*, 40(3).

Chapter 10

1. *'Using emotional and psychological strategies that ignore or make fun of a teenager's autonomy and preferences is directly connected to the development of depression, not resilience.'* Skinner, A.T., Çiftçi, L., Jones, S., Klotz, E., Ondrušková, T., Lansford, J.E., Alampay, L.P., Al-Hassan, S.M., Bacchini, D., Bornstein, M.H, Chang, L., Deater-Deckard, K., Di Giunta, L., Dodge, K.A., Gurdal, S., Liu, Q., Long, Q., Oburu, P., Pastorelli, C., …Yotanyamaneewong, S. (2022). 'Adolescent Positivity and Future Orientation, Parental Psychological Control, and Young Adult Internalising Behaviours during COVID-19 in Nine Countries.' *Social Sciences,* 11(75). https:// doi.org/10.3390/socsci11020075.

2. *'She inspired his own attitude to life …'* Radio interview, source unknown.

Chapter 11

1. *'Studies with sexual- and gender-diverse teenagers has found that self-compassion is particularly effective ...'* Vigna, A.J., Poehlmann-Tynan, J. & Koenig, B.W. (2017) 'Does Self-Compassion Facilitate Resilience to Stigma? A School-Based Study of Sexual and Gender Minority Youth.' *Mindfulness,* 9, 914–924. https://doi.org/10.1007/s12671-017-0831-x.

Chapter 13

1. *'Its founder Dr Garry Landreth is an internationally renowned play therapy expert and author. He once stated: 'Toys are used like words by ...'* Landreth, G.L. (2012). *Play Therapy: The art of the relationship. Third Edition.* Brunner-Routledge, New York.

Chapter 16

1. *This work is particularly relevant to the study of mindfulness ...* Epel, E., Daubenmier, J., Moskowitz, J.T., Folkman, S., & Blackburn, E. (2009). 'Can meditation slow rate of cellular aging? Cognitive stress, mindfulness, and telomeres.' *Annals of the New York Academy of Science.* Aug;1172:34-53. doi: 10.1111/j.1749-6632.2009.04414.x. PMID: 19735238; PMCID: PMC3057175.

2. *'As they were all focused on the passing of the ball ...'* Simons, D.J., & Chabris, C.F. (1999). 'Gorillas in our midst: Sustained inattentional blindness for dynamic events.' *Perception,* 28(9), 1059–1074. https://doi.org/10.1068/p281059.

Index

Index